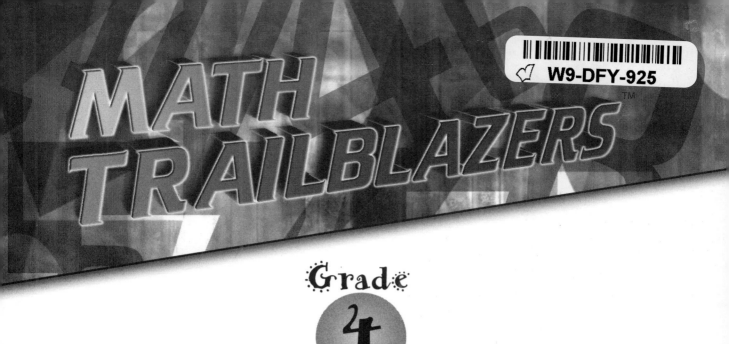

MATH TRAILBLAZERS™

Grade 4

Unit Resource Guide
Unit 5
Using Data to Predict

SECOND EDITION

A Mathematical Journey Using Science and Language Arts

KENDALL/HUNT PUBLISHING COMPANY
4050 Westmark Drive   Dubuque, Iowa 52002

A TIMS® Curriculum
University of Illinois at Chicago

UIC The University of Illinois
at Chicago

The original edition was based on work supported by the National Science Foundation under grant No. MDR 9050226 and the University of Illinois at Chicago. Any opinions, findings, and conclusions or recommendations expressed in this publication are those of the author(s) and do not necessarily reflect the views of the granting agencies.

LETTER HOME

Using Data to Predict

Date: _____

Dear Family Member:

In this unit, your child's class will make predictions using graphs and patterns in data.

We will also conduct an experiment called *Bouncing Ball*. Patterns in the *Bouncing Ball* data will allow us to make predictions about how high a ball will bounce when dropped from a given height. While making these predictions, students will solve problems and use math in much the same way as it is used in science, technology, and the business world.

Help your child at home by asking about his or her predictions.

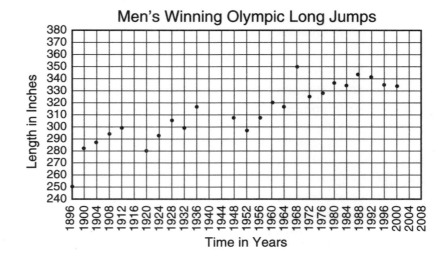

- Ask your child to tell you the story of the graph shown here. Predict the length of the winning long jump for the next Summer Olympic Games.

- Encourage your child to tell you about the *Bouncing Ball* lab. What data did his or her group collect? What predictions did the group make?

- In this unit, we continue reviewing the multiplication facts focusing on the third group of facts, the square numbers ($3 \times 3 = 9$, $4 \times 4 = 16$, $5 \times 5 = 25$, etc.). Your child can practice these facts using *Triangle Flash Cards*.

Thank you for your continued interest in your child's mathematical explorations.

Sincerely,

_____

Using Data to Predict

Pacing Suggestions

Students' knowledge of averages and familiarity with best-fit lines will determine how quickly the class can proceed through this unit. Use the smaller of the recommended number of sessions if students worked with these concepts and skills in third grade. Students will have numerous opportunities to use averages and draw and interpret best-fit lines in laboratory investigations, Daily Practice and Problems items, and Home Practice assignments in this and subsequent units. The unit includes two optional lessons:

- Lesson 5 *Two Heads Are Better Than One* is an *Adventure Book* story about two students who work together to correct a mistake in their graphs. Students can be challenged to find the mistake as they read the story. This lesson can be used as an extension.

- The second optional lesson, Lesson 7 *Speeds at the Indianapolis 500,* is a set of word problems that reviews concepts and skills developed in this and preceding units. It can be distributed as homework throughout the unit or used as an in-class review.

Math Trailblazers™ includes many connections to other subjects, especially science and language arts. Linking appropriate lessons with your instruction in other subjects can help maximize available time to complete lessons. For example, consider using some science time to collect data for the *Bouncing Ball* lab in Lesson 4. The *Adventure Book* story can be linked with language arts.

Components Key: SG = Student Guide, DAB = Discovery Assignment Book, AB = Adventure Book, URG = Unit Resource Guide, and DPP = Daily Practice and Problems

	Sessions	Description	Supplies
LESSON 1 **Predictions from Graphs** SG pages 120–124 DAB pages 59–64 URG pages 20–35 DPP A–D	2	**ACTIVITY:** Students look for patterns in point graphs. When appropriate, they draw best-fit lines and make predictions based on the graphs.	• rulers • envelopes
LESSON 2 **Another Average Activity** SG pages 125–131 URG pages 36–45 DPP E–F	1–2	**ACTIVITY:** Students investigate averages. Using manipulatives, they learn to find the mean and review how to find the median value of a set of data.	• square-inch tiles or connecting cubes • small paper bags

	Sessions	Description	Supplies
LESSON 3 **The Meaning of the Mean** SG pages 132–138 URG pages 46–55 DPP G–J	2–3	**ACTIVITY:** Students continue to explore averages. They find the circumferences of their classmates' heads and represent the data using means. First they use strips of adding machine tape to model the procedure for finding the mean, and then they use calculators. **ASSESSMENT PAGE:** *Cookie Factory,* Unit Resource Guide, page 54.	• adding machine tape or ball of string • metersticks • calculators • scissors • tape • rulers • crayons
LESSON 4 **Bouncing Ball** SG pages 139–145 URG pages 56–70 DPP K–R	4–5	**LAB:** Students look for the relationship between the drop height and the bounce height of a tennis ball and a Super ball. They collect, record, and graph the data, using the data to make predictions.	• tennis balls • Super balls • metersticks • masking tape • rulers
LESSON 5 		– OPTIONAL LESSON –	
Two Heads Are Better Than One AB pages 15–28 URG pages 71–76	1	**OPTIONAL ADVENTURE BOOK:** In this story, two students work together to complete the *Bouncing Ball* experiment. They arrive at different answers to a question from the lab, then they work cooperatively to solve the problem.	
LESSON 6 **Professor Peabody Invents a Ball** URG pages 77–89 DPP S–T	1–2	**ASSESSMENT ACTIVITY:** Students solve problems similar to those posed in the *Bouncing Ball* lab. They use the Student Rubrics: *Solving* and *Telling* to guide their work. **ASSESSMENT PAGE:** *Professor Peabody Invents a Ball,* Unit Resource Guide, page 88.	• rulers • calculators
LESSON 7 		– OPTIONAL ACTIVITY –	
Speeds at the Indianapolis 500 SG pages 146–148 URG pages 90–93	1	**OPTIONAL ACTIVITY:** Students solve word problems based on a graph that gives the average speeds of the winners of the Indianapolis 500 since 1911.	• rulers

	Sessions	Description	Supplies
LESSON 8 **Midterm Test** URG pages 94–102 DPP U–V	1	**ASSESSMENT ACTIVITY:** Students take a short-item test that assesses skills and concepts studied in the first four units. **ASSESSMENT PAGES:** *Midterm Test,* Unit Resource Guide, pages 97–101.	• rulers • square-inch tiles • calculators

CONNECTIONS

A current list of connections is available at www.mathtrailblazers.com.

Software
- *Graph Master* provides practice with collecting data and creating graphs.
- *Kid Pix* helps students create their own illustrations.
- *Math Mysteries Measurement* provides practice with multistep problem solving involving distance, weight, and capacity.

PREPARING FOR UPCOMING LESSONS

In an optional lesson in Unit 6, students will fill jars with objects and estimate the number of objects in the jars. Begin asking students to collect jars from home.

In Unit 6, students will cut out articles that use big numbers from newspapers and magazines. Begin collecting newspapers and magazines for students.

UNIT 5 BACKGROUND

Using Data to Predict

In this unit, students use data from different sources to make predictions. For example, using a graph of data from past Olympic contests and studying the patterns in the data, they make predictions about contests in future Olympics. Several new ideas are introduced in the unit that help students become more sophisticated in their skills with data collection and analysis. They begin using the terms manipulated, responding, and fixed to describe variables in a controlled scientific experiment. While these terms will be new, the concepts that underlie them have been used by students in previous grades in laboratory experiments. We will continue to use these terms in many experiments. Students will have ample opportunities to gain confidence and facility in the use of this new vocabulary.

Best-fit lines. Students further explore the use of best-fit lines to make predictions from graphs. Drawing best-fit lines is done here simply by eye. The technique of fitting lines to data is frequently used by mathematicians and scientists to analyze data.

For more information on best-fit lines or manipulated, responding, and fixed variables, see the TIMS Tutor: *The TIMS Laboratory Method* in the *Teacher Implementation Guide.*

Averages. In this unit, we review the use of medians as averages and introduce a second kind of average, the mean. Use of the mean provides students with another tool for finding a representative value for a data set. The concept is first introduced concretely, through the use of cubes and measure-ment. Students then practice finding means using a calculator. See the TIMS Tutor: *Averages* in the *Teacher Implementation Guide* for a more detailed discussion.

Bouncing Ball lab. This lab is the centerpiece of the unit and integrates many of the skills and concepts students have learned in previous units and previous grades. Students use the four steps of the TIMS Laboratory Method to collect and display interesting data about how high a ball will bounce. Within the context of the lab, they use a best-fit line drawn on the graph to make predictions from the data. They use patterns in the data table and the graph to solve problems involving proportional reasoning. They utilize their problem-solving skills to solve problems in the lab.

Assessment. After completing the *Bouncing Ball* lab, students use similar data to solve an open-ended problem, *Professor Peabody Invents a Ball.* As part of this activity, students are introduced to the Student Rubric: *Solving.* Their responses to the problems in this activity should be included in their portfolios. For more information about the *TIMS Multidimensional Rubric,* see the Assessment section in the *Teacher Implementation Guide.*

Math Facts. The systematic review and practice of the math facts continues in this unit with the square numbers. Students use *Triangle Flash Cards* to practice these multiplication facts. They will study the division facts through the use of fact families.

Resources

- Korithoski, Theodor P., and Patricia A. "Mean or Meaningless?" in *The Arithmetic Teacher*. The National Council of Teachers of Mathematics, Reston, VA, December 1993, pp. 194–197.
- Matsumoto, A.N. "Correlation, Junior Varsity Style." In A.P. Shulte and J.R. Smart (Eds.), *Teaching Statistics and Probability: 1981 Yearbook*. The National Council of Teachers of Mathematics, Reston, VA, 1981.
- Wallechinsky, D. *The Complete Book of the Summer Olympics*. The Overlook Press, New York, 2000.

Assessment Indicators

- Can students draw and interpret best-fit lines?
- Can students find the median and mean of a data set?
- Can students identify and use variables?
- Can students measure length in centimeters?
- Can students use patterns in data tables and graphs to make predictions?
- Can students collect, organize, graph, and analyze data?
- Can students solve open-response problems and communicate solution strategies?
- Do students demonstrate fluency with the multiplication facts for the square numbers?
- Can students write the two number sentences in the fact families for the square numbers?

OBSERVATIONAL ASSESSMENT RECORD

(A1) Can students draw and interpret best-fit lines?

(A2) Can students find the median and mean of a data set?

(A3) Can students identify and use variables?

(A4) Can students measure length in centimeters?

(A5) Can students use patterns in data tables and graphs to make predictions?

(A6) Can students collect, organize, graph, and analyze data?

(A7) Can students solve open-response problems and communicate solution strategies?

(A8) Do students demonstrate fluency with the multiplication facts for the square numbers?

(A9) Can students write the two number sentences in the fact families for the square numbers?

(A10) _____

Name	A1	A2	A3	A4	A5	A6	A7	A8	A9	A10	Comments
1.											
2.											
3.											
4.											
5.											
6.											
7.											
8.											
9.											
10.											
11.											
12.											
13.											

Name	A1	A2	A3	A4	A5	A6	A7	A8	A9	A10	Comments
14.											
15.											
16.											
17.											
18.											
19.											
20.											
21.											
22.											
23.											
24.											
25.											
26.											
27.											
28.											
29.											
30.											
31.											
32.											

Daily Practice and Problems

Using Data to Predict

Two Daily Practice and Problems (DPP) items are included for each nonoptional class session listed in the Unit Outline. The first item is always a Bit and the second is either a Task or a Challenge. Refer to the Daily Practice and Problems and Home Practice Guide in the *Teacher Implementation Guide* for further information on the DPP. A Scope and Sequence Chart for the DPP for the year can be found in the Scope and Sequence Chart & the NCTM *Principles and Standards* section of the *Teacher Implementation Guide*.

A DPP Menu for Unit 5

Eight icons designate the subject matter of the DPP items. Each DPP item may fall into one or more of the categories listed below. A brief menu of the DPP items included in Unit 5 follows.

N Number Sense	**✖** Computation	**🕒** Time	**▱** Geometry
B–E, H, M, P–R, T, V	D–G, J, R, V	F	K, L
⁵⁄ₓ₇ Math Facts	**$** Money	**🔢** Measurement	**◿** Data
A, B, G–J, L, N, P, T, U	J	K, L	M, O, Q–S

The Multiplication and Division Facts

By the end of fourth grade, students in *Math Trailblazers* are expected to demonstrate fluency with all the multiplication and division facts. The DPP for this unit continues the systematic, strategies-based approach to practicing the multiplication facts and learning the division facts through the use of fact families and other strategies. This unit focuses on the third group of facts, the square numbers.

The *Triangle Flash Cards: Square Numbers* follow the Home Practice for this unit in the *Discovery Assignment Book*. In Grade 4, students use the flash cards to practice the multiplication facts through Unit 8. In Units 9 through 16, students use the *Triangle Flash Cards* to practice the division facts. Bit A of the DPP for Unit 5 contains instructions for using the *Triangle Flash Cards* and the *Multiplication Facts I Know* chart. DPP Bit U is a quiz on the square numbers multiplication facts. Each of the other items listed under the Math Facts icon in the DPP menu provides practice using the multiplication and division facts for the square numbers.

Students may solve the items individually, in groups, or as a class. The items may also be assigned for homework.

Student Questions	Teacher Notes

A **Triangle Flash Cards: Square Numbers**

With a partner, use your *Triangle Flash Cards* to quiz each other on the multiplication facts for the square numbers. One partner covers the shaded corner containing the highest number. This number will be the answer to a multiplication fact called the product. The second person multiplies the other two numbers. These two are the factors.

Separate the used cards into three piles: those facts you know and can answer quickly, those that you can figure out with a strategy, and those that you need to learn. Practice the last two piles again and then make a list of the facts you need to practice at home for homework.

Circle the facts you know and can answer quickly on your *Multiplication Facts I Know* chart.

TIMS Bit

The *Triangle Flash Cards* follow the Home Practice for this unit in the *Discovery Assignment Book*. Part 1 of the Home Practice reminds students to bring the list of the facts they need to practice home for homework. The *Triangle Flash Cards* should also be sent home.

Have students circle the facts they know well on their *Multiplication Facts I Know* charts. Remind students that if they know a fact, they also know its turn-around fact. Since these charts can also be used as multiplication tables, students should have them available to use as needed.

Inform students when the quiz on the square numbers will be given. This quiz appears in TIMS Bit U.

Student Questions	Teacher Notes

 Guess My Number

I am a multiple of 3.

2 is not one of my factors.

I am not a prime and I am not a square.

I am less than 20.

What number am I?

Explain your strategy.

TIMS Task

15

All multiples of 3: 3, 6, 9, 12, 15, 18, 21, 24, 27, 30, etc.

Eliminate factors of 2, leaving 3, 9, 15, 21, 27, etc.

Eliminate prime numbers and square numbers, leaving 15, 21, 27, etc.

Only one number above is less than 20: 15.

 Base-Ten Pieces

1. Write 4318 using base-ten shorthand.

2. What is the value of the 3 in 4318?

TIMS Bit

1. Answers may vary. The solution shown uses the fewest pieces.

2. 3 hundred

 Addition and Subtraction Practice

1. 3067
    + 484

2. 8905
    − 1266

3. $39 + n = 72$

4. $82 − 45 = n$

5. $102 − n = 4$

6. $n + 93 + 22 = 120$

TIMS Task

1. 3551
2. 7639
3. 33
4. 37
5. 98
6. 5

 Finding Prime Factors

Write 90 as the product of prime numbers.

TIMS Bit

Suggest that students create a factor tree to find the prime factors for 90.

$90 = 2 \times 3 \times 3 \times 5$

Cooking a Turkey

Roberto's mother put a turkey in the oven at 11:30. The instructions say that the turkey should cook about 17 minutes per pound. The turkey weighs 20 pounds.

1. About how long should Roberto's mother cook the turkey?

2. About what time will the turkey be ready?

3. Roberto's mother decided that the turkey was ready at 5:20. How long did the turkey cook?

TIMS Challenge

1. 17 minutes per pound is about an hour for every 4 pounds; between 5 and 6 hours for 20 pounds (17 minutes per pound × 20 pounds = 340 minutes or 5 hours and 40 minutes)

2. about 5:00 or 5:30

3. 5 hours, 50 minutes

 Using Exponents

A. $2^2 = ?$ B. $3^2 = ?$

C. $2^2 + 3^2 = ?$ D. $4^2 = ?$

E. $3^2 \times 5 = ?$ F. $2 \times 4^2 = ?$

TIMS Bit

Students should use exponents before they add or multiply. For example, $2^2 + 3^2 = 4 + 9 = 13$.

A. 4   B. 9

C. 13   D. 16

E. 45   F. 32

H **Number Puzzle**

I am a square number less than 100.

I am a multiple of 2, but I am not a multiple of 8.

2 is not my only prime factor.

What number am I?

Explain your strategy.

TIMS Task

36

Square numbers less than 100: 1, 4, 9, 16, 25, 36, 49, 64, 81

Numbers from the list above that are multiples of 2, but not of 8: 4 and 36

The only prime factor of 4 is 2.

Prime factors of 36: 2 and 3, so the answer is 36.

Fact Families for the Square Numbers

TIMS Bit

The square numbers have only two facts in each fact family.

For example, the following two facts are in the same fact family.

$$2 \times 2 = 4 \text{ and } 4 \div 2 = 2$$

Solve the fact given. Then, name the second fact that is in the same fact family.

1. $9 \times 9 =$ _____   2. $5 \times 5 =$ _____

3. $7 \times 7 =$ _____   4. $8 \times 8 =$ _____

5. $10 \times 10 =$ _____   6. $3 \times 3 =$ _____

7. $6 \times 6 =$ _____   8. $4 \times 4 =$ _____

9. $1 \times 1 =$ _____

1. $81; 81 \div 9 = 9$
2. $25; 25 \div 5 = 5$
3. $49; 49 \div 7 = 7$
4. $64; 64 \div 8 = 8$
5. $100; 100 \div 10 = 10$
6. $9; 9 \div 3 = 3$
7. $36; 36 \div 6 = 6$
8. $16; 16 \div 4 = 4$
9. $1; 1 \div 1 = 1$

Grocery Shopping

TIMS Task

1. Paper towels cost 70¢ a roll. How much will 7 rolls cost?

2. Turkey sandwiches cost $2.50. How much will 3 sandwiches cost?

3. Frozen yogurt cups cost 59¢ apiece. About how much will 6 cups cost?

4. A juice pack has 3 juice boxes. A juice pack costs $0.90. How much is each juice box worth?

1. $4.90
2. $7.50
3. About $3.60
4. $0.30

Drawing Angles

Draw an acute angle, a right angle, an obtuse angle, and a 180° angle. Then, switch with a partner and see if he or she can tell which is which.

TIMS Bit

Some right angles:

Remind students that they can check for a right angle using the corner of a sheet of paper.

The size of the acute angle and obtuse angle may vary. Sample drawings are shown here.

An acute angle:

An obtuse angle:

A 180° angle:

 Area and Perimeter

1. Imagine a rectangle with 7 rows of square-inch tiles. Each row has 7 tiles in it.

    A. What is the area of this rectangle?

    B. What is the perimeter? Make a sketch of this rectangle.

2. Imagine a square with perimeter of 32 inches. What is the area of this square? Make a sketch of this square.

TIMS Task

1. A. 49 square inches

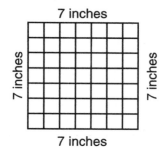

B. 28 inches

2. 64 square inches

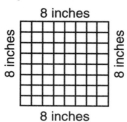

Median

Six students grabbed a handful of cubes. They pulled 10, 12, 10, 11, 15, and 14 cubes.

1. What is the median number of cubes in a handful?

2. What is the mean?

TIMS Bit

Students found the median and mean of such data in *Another Average Activity* (Lesson 2) in this unit.

1. 11.5 cubes (An answer of "11 or 12 cubes" is also acceptable.)

2. 12 cubes

 Square Numbers

Find a number for *n* that makes each sentence true.

1. $n \times n = 81$ $n = \underline{\quad}$

2. $n \times n = 36$ $n = \underline{\quad}$

3. $n \times n = 49$ $n = \underline{\quad}$

4. $n \times n = 25$ $n = \underline{\quad}$

5. $n \times n = 9$ $n = \underline{\quad}$

6. $n \times n = 64$ $n = \underline{\quad}$

7. $n \times n = 16$ $n = \underline{\quad}$

8. $n \times n = 1$ $n = \underline{\quad}$

9. $n \times n = 4$ $n = \underline{\quad}$

TIMS Task

Explain to students that in each sentence both *n*s have to have the same value.

1. $n = 9$

2. $n = 6$

3. $n = 7$

4. $n = 5$

5. $n = 3$

6. $n = 8$

7. $n = 4$

8. $n = 1$

9. $n = 2$

Bouncing Balls

Ming experimented with 3 kinds of balls to find which one bounced the highest. He chose a basketball, a tennis ball, and a kickball. He dropped each ball from 1 meter and measured the bounce height.

1. What is the manipulated variable in Ming's experiment?

2. What is the responding variable?

3. Is the responding variable numerical or categorical?

4. What are the values of the manipulated variable?

5. Name one fixed variable.

TIMS Bit

1. kind of ball

2. bounce height

3. numerical variable

4. basketball, tennis ball, and kickball

5. Answers will vary. drop height (1 meter), person dropping the ball, the surface on which the balls are dropped

---

P Another Number Puzzle

I am a number between 6 and 150.

I am one more than a square number.

The sum of my digits is a multiple of 5.

I am prime.

What number am I?

Explain your strategy.

TIMS Challenge

37

Square numbers between 6–150: 9, 16, 25, 36, 49, 64, 81, 100, 121, 144

Numbers one larger than the squares above (between 6 and 150): 10, 17, 26, 37, 50, 65, 82, 101, 122, 145

Numbers from the list above whose digits sum to a multiple of five:

37 (3 + 7 = 10),

50 (5 + 0 = 5),

82, 122, 145

Of these numbers, only 37 is a prime number. The others are divisible by 2 or 5.

Q Finding Medians

In third grade, Luis did an experiment called *Fill 'er Up.* He measured the volume of three different containers.

C Container	*V* Volume (in cc)			
	Trial 1	Trial 2	Trial 3	Median
Salsa	750 cc	755 cc	760 cc	
Baby Food	98 cc	118 cc	115 cc	
Mayonnaise	1010 cc	1020 cc	1012 cc	

Find the median volume for each container.

TIMS Bit

This item provides practice for finding the median (middle) value of three trials. Students will use this skill in many labs.

Container	Median
Salsa	755 cc
Baby Food	115 cc
Mayonnaise	1012 cc

R Finding Means

In third grade, Luis did an experiment called *Fill 'er Up.* He measured the volume of three different containers.

C Container	*V* Volume (in cc)			
	Trial 1	Trial 2	Trial 3	Mean
Salsa	750 cc	755 cc	760 cc	
Baby Food	98 cc	118 cc	115 cc	
Mayonnaise	1010 cc	1020 cc	1012 cc	

Use a calculator to find the mean volume for each container. Give your answer to the nearest cubic centimeter. Look back at your answers. Are they reasonable?

TIMS Task

This item provides practice for finding the mean value of three trials. Students should add the three trials and divide by 3. They will use this skill in many labs. They should decide if their answers are reasonable.

Container	Mean
Salsa	755 cc
Baby Food	110 cc
Mayonnaise	1014 cc

Paper Towels

When Jackie was in the third grade, she did an experiment with paper towels. She dropped water on one sheet of three different brands of paper towels (Ecotowel, Cheap-O, and Handy). She dropped three drops of water on each towel. The water spread out and made a spot. Jackie then measured the area of each spot of water in square centimeters.

1. What is the manipulated variable? What is the responding variable?

2. What are the values of the manipulated variable?

3. Is the manipulated variable numerical or categorical?

4. Name one fixed variable.

TIMS Bit

1. The manipulated variable is the brand of paper towel. The responding variable is the area of the spot.

2. The values of the manipulated variable are Ecotowel, Cheap-O, and Handy.

3. categorical

4. Answers will vary. One fixed variable is the number of drops.

 Missing Factors

m and n stand for missing numbers. Find the missing numbers in each of the following.

1. $2 \times m = 4$

2. $m \times 8 = 24$

3. $6 \times m = 36$

4. $10 \times m = 100$

5. $64 \div m = 8$

6. $81 \div 9 = m$

7. $4 \times n = 16$

8. $m \times n = 11$

9. $m^2 = 25$

TIMS Task

1. 2   2. 3

3. 6   4. 10

5. 8   6. 9

7. 4   8. 1, 11

9. 5

Student Questions	Teacher Notes

 Quiz on the Square Numbers

A. $4 \times 4 =$ B. $7 \times 7 =$

C. $2 \times 2 =$ D. $10 \times 10 =$

E. $3 \times 3 =$ F. $5 \times 5 =$

G. $6 \times 6 =$ H. $8 \times 8 =$

I. $9 \times 9 =$ J. $1 \times 1 =$

TIMS Bit

This quiz is on the third group of multiplication facts, the square numbers. We recommend 1 minute for this test. Allow students to change pens after the time is up and complete the remaining problems in a different color.

After students take the test, have them update their *Multiplication Facts I Know* charts.

Biggest and Smallest Sums

Put a digit (1, 2, 3, 4, 5, 6, 7, 8, 9, or 0) in each box. Use each digit once or not at all.

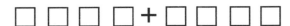

What is the biggest sum you can make?

What is the smallest?

What if a digit can be used more than once?

Explain your strategies.

TIMS Challenge

The largest sum is
9753 + 8642 = 18,395.
The smallest sum is
1046 + 2357 = 3403
(or 1357 + 0246 = 1603
if leading zeros are allowed).
Other addends may give the
same sums and are also correct.

If repeated digits are allowed,
the largest sum is 9999 +
9999 = 19,998. The smallest
sum is 1000 + 1000 = 2000.
If leading zeros are allowed,
then the smallest sum is
0000 + 0000 = 0.

Daily Practice and Problems: Bits for Lesson 1

A. Triangle Flash Cards:
   Square Numbers (URG p. 10)

With a partner, use your *Triangle Flash Cards* to quiz each other on the multiplication facts for the square numbers. One partner covers the shaded corner containing the highest number. This number will be the answer to a multiplication fact called the product. The second person multiplies the other two numbers. These two are the factors.

Separate the used cards into three piles: those facts you know and can answer quickly, those that you can figure out with a strategy, and those that you need to learn. Practice the last two piles again and then make a list of the facts you need to practice at home for homework.

Circle the facts you know and can answer quickly on your *Multiplication Facts I Know* chart.

C. Base Ten Pieces (URG p. 11)

1. Write 4318 using base-ten shorthand.

2. What is the value of the 3 in 4318?

DPP Tasks are on page 27. Suggestions for using the DPPs are on page 27.

Predictions from Graphs

Estimated Class Sessions: 2

Students look for patterns in point graphs and use these patterns to make predictions. If the data points suggest a line, they draw a best-fit line and use the line to make predictions about the data.

Key Content

- Using patterns in graphs to make predictions about data.
- Drawing and interpreting best-fit lines.
- Connecting mathematics to real-world situations.

Key Vocabulary

best-fit line
extrapolation
interpolation

Curriculum Sequence

Before This Unit

Best-Fit Lines. Students were introduced to best-fit lines in Grade 3 Unit 9 and used lines to make predictions in succeeding units. In Grade 4 Unit 2, students made point graphs with exact data and drew lines through the points.

After This Unit

Best-Fit Lines. Students will continue to use best-fit lines to make predictions in labs in Units 8, 10, 15, and 16.

Materials List

Print Materials for Students

	Math Facts and Daily Practice and Problems	Activity	Homework
Student Books			
Student Guide		*Predictions from Graphs* Pages 120–124	
Discovery Assignment Book		*Using Best-Fit Lines* Pages 59–64	Home Practice Parts 1 & 5 Pages 53 & 55 and *Triangle Flash Cards: Square Numbers* Page 57
Teacher Resources			
Facts Resource Guide ◎	DPP Items 5A & 5B Use *Triangle Flash Cards: Square Numbers* to review the multiplication facts for the square numbers.		
Unit Resource Guide	DPP Items A–D Pages 10–11 ◎		

◎ available on Teacher Resource CD

All Transparency Masters, Blackline Masters, and Assessment Blackline Masters in the Unit Resource Guide are on the Teacher Resource CD.

Supplies for Each Student

ruler
string or uncooked spaghetti, optional
envelopes for storing flash cards

Materials for the Teacher

Olympic Long Jump Transparency Master (Unit Resource Guide) Page 30
Mile Run Transparency Master (Unit Resource Guide) Page 31
Nila's Sit-Ups Transparency Master (Unit Resource Guide) Page 32
Observational Assessment Record (Unit Resource Guide, Pages 7–8 and Teacher Resource CD)

Predictions from Graphs

Graphs can tell stories. The following graph tells a story about the men's long jump competition in the Olympics. Contestants in the long jump try to jump as far as possible with a running start.

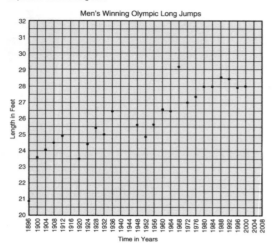

1. A. What variable is on the horizontal axis?
   B. What variable is on the vertical axis?

　　　Predictions from Graphs

Student Guide - Page 120

2. Jesse Owens won the long jump competition in 1936.
   A. How far did he jump?
   B. Is the distance Jesse Owens jumped longer or shorter than the length of your classroom?
   C. How many years passed before someone jumped farther than Jesse Owens in the Olympics?

3. A. Describe the graph. What does it look like?
   B. If you read the graph from left to right, do the points tend to go uphill or downhill?
   C. What does the graph tell you about the winning long jumps in the Olympics?

4. In 1968 Bob Beamon of the United States won the long jump competition.
   A. How far did Beamon jump?
   B. What is unusual about this point on the graph?
   C. Do you think the winner in 2008 will jump as far as Bob Beamon jumped in 1968? Why or why not?

Student Guide - Page 121

Developing the Activity

This activity is divided into two parts. First, the class looks for patterns and makes predictions using graphs found in the *Predictions from Graphs* Activity Pages in the *Student Guide*. In the second part, students practice drawing best-fit lines and making predictions using the *Using Best-Fit Lines* Activity Pages in the *Discovery Assignment Book*.

TIMS Tip
To increase student participation, give student pairs or groups a minute to talk about each question before the question is discussed by the whole class.

Part 1. Predictions from Graphs

This activity begins with a discussion of the graph, Men's Winning Olympic Long Jumps, on the *Predictions from Graphs* Activity Pages in the *Student Guide*. (Display the *Olympic Long Jump* Transparency Master as you lead the discussion.) The graph charts the winning long jumps in the Olympics from 1896 to 2000. *Questions 1–2* orient students to the graph. *Question 3* asks students to describe the graph. Students often say that the graph "looks like mountains" or that the graph is "bumpy." To refine their descriptions of the graph, ask:

• *What can you say about the points as you look from left to right on the graph? What does that tell you about the winning long jumps?*

It is important to note that the points tend to go uphill from left to right on the graph. This indicates that usually we can expect the length of the long jumps to increase from one Olympics to the next. Students may see other interesting trends in the data. (See the Social Studies Connection at the end of this Lesson Guide.)

Question 4 asks about the winning jump in 1968. Bob Beamon jumped more than 29 feet. This was more than two feet longer than any previous jump, which is very unusual. Following the pattern of the data points since 1896, we can predict that Beamon's record might be broken by 2008. However, if we just consider data points since 1972, we would probably not make this prediction.

The second graph shows winning times for the mile run in the Men's National Collegiate Championships from 1921 until 1975 when the race became 1500 meters instead of the mile. Use the *Mile Run Transparency Master* to guide class discussion. *Questions 5–7* are provided as a check to see if students can read the graph. Be sure they can read the minutes and seconds on the vertical axis before continuing the discussion. *Question 8* asks students to describe the graph. Students will likely respond with many observations including the idea that the points form a "bumpy" line that "goes downhill." That tells us that the winning time for running the mile decreased over the years.

Question 9 introduces students to **best-fit lines.** This is the line that fits the points as closely as possible. It indicates the direction of the points. You can demonstrate how to draw the best-fit line on the transparency using a piece of string or a clear ruler. One teacher recommends using a piece of spaghetti to demonstrate drawing a best-fit line. *Questions 9B–9D* emphasize that the best-fit line may not go through many of the points, but usually about the same number of points should lie on either side of the line. It is important to clarify that the best-fit line is always a straight line. Students sometimes are tempted to see it as the line that connects the dots.

Question 10 asks for an estimation of the winning time in 1955. There is no data point here, but following the best-fit line, we can estimate that the winning time that year was probably between four minutes and five seconds and four minutes and ten seconds. *Question 11* asks for a prediction for the winning time in the year 2005. This is harder to do since it is outside the range of our data. The pattern of the points suggests that if the mile were run in 2005, then the winning time would be near three minutes and 45 seconds. Other predictions are possible depending on the interpretation of the data.

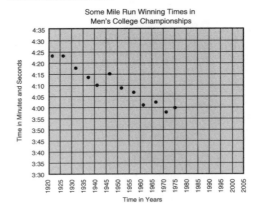

Here is another graph. It shows the history of the mile run in college championship races. Runners do not run the mile anymore in these track meets because the distances are measured using the metric system. Contestants now run 1500 meters, which is a little shorter than a mile.

5. A. What variable is on the horizontal axis?
   B. What variable is on the vertical axis?

6. What was the winning time for running the mile in 1941?

7. Find the data point which shows a time for the mile race which is less than 4 minutes. What is the year for this data point?

8. A. Describe the graph. What does it look like?
   B. If you read the graph from left to right, do the points tend to go uphill or downhill?
   C. What does the graph tell you about the winning times for the mile run?

Predictions from Graphs

Student Guide - Page 122

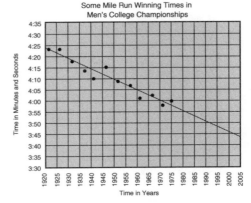

If the points on a graph lie close to a line, you can draw a line to help you make predictions. This line is called the **best-fit line.**

9. A. Why do you think the line drawn on the graph is called a best-fit line?
   B. How many points on the graph are above the line?
   C. How many points are on the line?
   D. How many points are below the line?

10. Use this graph to estimate the winning time for the mile run in 1955.

11. If the mile were run in the college championships in the year 2005, predict the winning time. Explain how you made your prediction.

Predictions from Graphs

Student Guide - Page 123

12. **A.** Did you use interpolation or extrapolation to estimate the winning time in 1955?

    B. Did you use interpolation or extrapolation to predict the winning time in 2005?

    C. Which is more accurate? Explain.

Student Guide - Page 124

Name _____ Date _____

Using Best-Fit Lines

1. Each year, Mrs. Welch, a gym teacher at Bessie Coleman School, records the number of sit-ups each student can do. Nila used her data to make a graph which shows the number of sit-ups she could do each year.

    A. Describe the graph.

    B. If you read the graph from left to right, do the points go uphill or downhill?

    C. What does the graph tell you about the number of sit-ups Nila can do?

    D. Do the points lie close to a straight line? If so, use a ruler to draw a best-fit line.

    E. If possible, predict the number of sit-ups Nila will be able to do when she is 12.

    F. Does knowing Nila's age help you predict the number of sit-ups she can do?

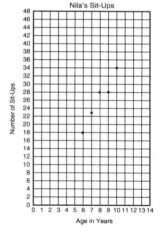

Discovery Assignment Book - Page 59

At this point, the text introduces the terms **interpolation** and **extrapolation,** and *Question 12* asks students to use the terms. Estimating data points that lie within the data as in *Question 10* is interpolating. Predicting data points that lie beyond the range of the data as in *Question 11* is extrapolating. Extrapolation is riskier since we cannot really know what will happen. Our prediction for the year 2005 may not be very accurate since we are so far beyond the range of the data.

Part 2. Using Best-Fit Lines

In the second part of the activity, students work individually to practice drawing best-fit lines and using them to make predictions. On the *Using Best-Fit Lines* Activity Pages in the *Discovery Assignment Book,* students will find six point graphs. They are asked to describe each graph. Encourage students to describe patterns in terms of lines or curves. Do the points tend to go uphill or downhill? If the points suggest a line, students should draw a best-fit line.

> ### Content Note
> Some students may raise a question about where a **best-fit line** that goes "uphill" should start. Should the line start at the origin, that is, at point (0,0)? Or, should students fit the line through the data points, extend it, and let it cross the vertical or horizontal axis wherever it falls? The answer depends on the data for the graph. For example, for the *Mass vs. Number of Cookies* graph, it makes sense that when the number of cookies is 0, the mass is 0 grams. The best-fit line for this graph should go through the origin (0 cookies, 0 grams). (See *Question 4* on the *Best-Fit Lines* Activity Pages in the *Discovery Assignment Book.*)
>
> On the other hand, the best-fit line for the Men's Winning Olympic Long Jumps graph will not go through the origin because the horizontal axis begins at the year 1896. Even if data were available back to the year zero, however, it would not make sense for the line to go through the origin because the length of the winning long jump in the year zero would have been greater than zero. Similarly, in the Head Circumference of Babies graph, if a curve were to be drawn, it should not go through the origin. When a baby is newborn (0 months old), the circumference of its head will not be zero. As the graph shows, it generally is about 35 centimeters. (See *Question 5* on the *Using Best-Fit Lines* Activity Pages.)

Use the *Nila's Sit-Ups* Transparency Master to model drawing a best-fit line. (See Figure 1.) Students can experiment with various angles using a ruler (preferably a clear ruler) or a piece of string. As a rule of thumb, to fit a line try to get about as many points above the line as below it. Once they have decided on the placement of the line, students should draw it using a pencil and a ruler. They should extend the line in both directions. Each student may draw the line a little bit differently. This will result in differing predictions. The lines and predictions, however, should be relatively close.

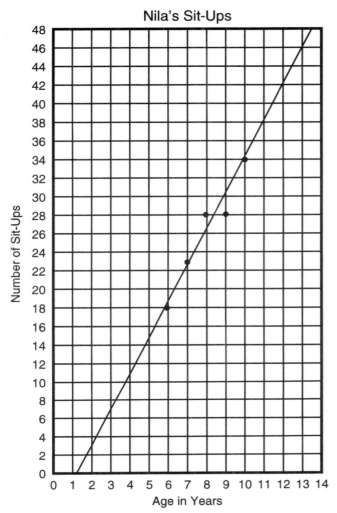

Figure 1: *Drawing a best-fit line*

The points on the graph in *Question 2* lie close to a line that goes downhill since John's times for running the mile decrease as he gets older. Students use extrapolation to predict John's time for running the mile when he is 12 to be about 7 minutes (*Question 2D*). If students use the best-fit line to predict John's time when he is 18 (*Question 2E*), the answers will probably vary since 18 years is so far beyond the last data point. They may say that his time will be about one or two minutes. This is not a reasonable prediction, however. *Question 2F* asks if knowing John's age helps predict his time for running a mile. Knowing his age helps only if we are talking about ages within or near the data points. As shown in this situation, extrapolating far beyond the actual data points is often unreliable and may be unreasonable.

The points on the graph in *Question 3* do not form a line. There is little relationship between the number

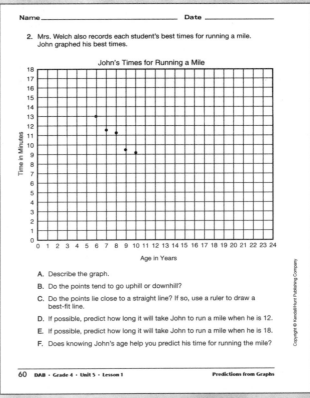

Discovery Assignment Book - Page 60

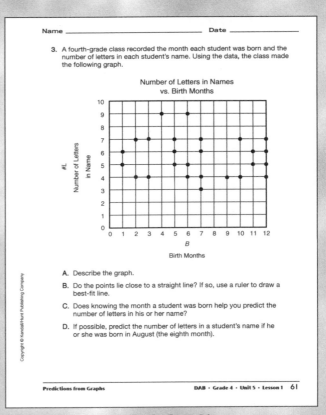

Discovery Assignment Book - Page 61

4. A cookie company wants all the cookies from the factory to be the same. Here is a graph made by a cookie inspector.

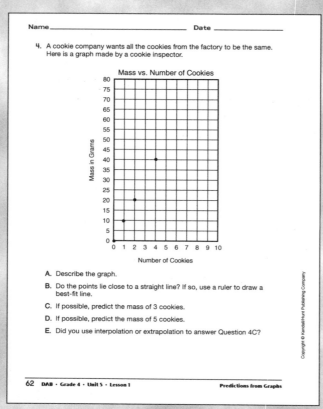

A. Describe the graph.

B. Do the points lie close to a straight line? If so, use a ruler to draw a best-fit line.

C. If possible, predict the mass of 3 cookies.

D. If possible, predict the mass of 5 cookies.

E. Did you use interpolation or extrapolation to answer Question 4C?

Discovery Assignment Book - Page 62

---

of letters in a person's name and that person's birth month. It would not make sense to draw a line on the graph. Although students may predict that the number of letters in a person's name is between three and nine letters, knowing the person's birth month will not help make a better prediction.

The points on the graph in **Question 4** lie directly on the line. However, the points in the graph in **Question 5** do not suggest a line, but they do form a curve. Even though it would not make sense to draw a best-fit line, it is possible to use the graph to predict the head circumference of a baby if you know the baby's age. Ask students why this graph shows a curve rather than a line. What would it mean if it were a line that kept going up?

Question 7 asks students to look back at the six graphs and tell which graph can be used to make the most accurate predictions. Since the points in the graph in **Question 4** lie directly on the line, this graph will most likely provide the most accurate information.

---

5. Doctors measure the head circumference of babies to track their growth.

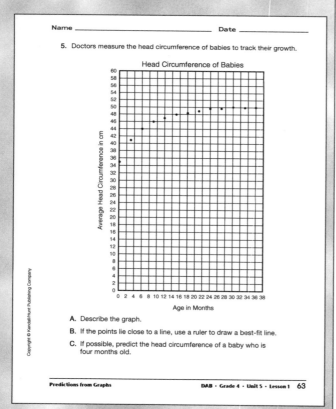

A. Describe the graph.

B. If the points lie close to a line, use a ruler to draw a best-fit line.

C. If possible, predict the head circumference of a baby who is four months old.

Discovery Assignment Book - Page 63

---

6. The winning times for the women's Olympic breaststroke swimming competition are shown in this graph.

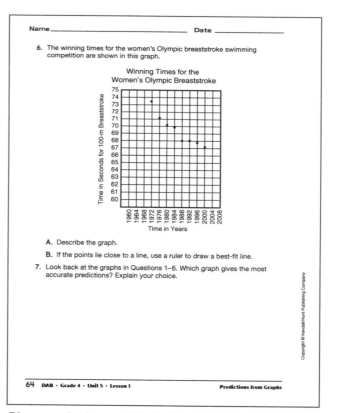

A. Describe the graph.

B. If the points lie close to a line, use a ruler to draw a best-fit line.

7. Look back at the graphs in Questions 1–6. Which graph gives the most accurate predictions? Explain your choice.

Discovery Assignment Book - Page 64

Suggestions for Teaching the Lesson

Math Facts

DPP Bit A and Home Practice Part 1 remind students to use the *Triangle Flash Cards* to practice the multiplication facts for the square numbers. Task B is a riddle that uses multiplication facts.

Homework and Practice

- DPP Bit C provides review of place value and base-ten shorthand. Task D provides multidigit addition and subtraction practice.
- Assign Parts 1 and 5 of the Home Practice.

Answers for Part 5 of the Home Practice can be found in the Answer Key at the end of this lesson and at the end of this unit.

Assessment

Observe students as they draw best-fit lines. Do they choose to draw the lines when it is appropriate? Do they use a ruler? Are there about as many points above the line as below? Use the *Observational Assessment Record* to record your observations.

Daily Practice and Problems: Tasks for Lesson 1

B. Task: Guess My Number
(URG p. 11)

I am a multiple of 3.

2 is not one of my factors.

I am not a prime and I am not a square.

I am less than 20.

What number am I?

Explain your strategy.

D. Task: Addition and Subtraction Practice (URG p. 11)

1.
```
   3067
 +  484
```

2.
```
   8905
 - 1266
```

3. $39 + n = 72$

4. $82 - 45 = n$

5. $102 - n = 4$

6. $n + 93 + 22 = 120$

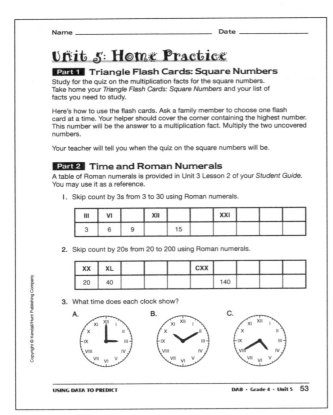

Name _____ Date _____

Unit 5: Home Practice

Part 1 Triangle Flash Cards: Square Numbers

Study for the quiz on the multiplication facts for the square numbers. Take home your *Triangle Flash Cards: Square Numbers* and your list of facts you need to study.

Here's how to use the flash cards. Ask a family member to choose one flash card at a time. Your helper should cover the corner containing the highest number. This number will be the answer to a multiplication fact. Multiply the two uncovered numbers.

Your teacher will tell you when the quiz on the square numbers will be.

Part 2 Time and Roman Numerals

A table of Roman numerals is provided in Unit 3 Lesson 2 of your *Student Guide*. You may use it as a reference.

1. Skip count by 3s from 3 to 30 using Roman numerals.

III	VI		XII		XXI			
3	6	9		15				

2. Skip count by 20s from 20 to 200 using Roman numerals.

XX	XL			CXX			
20	40				140		

3. What time does each clock show?

A.   B.   C.

USING DATA TO PREDICT   DAB · Grade 4 · Unit 5   53

Discovery Assignment Book - Page 53

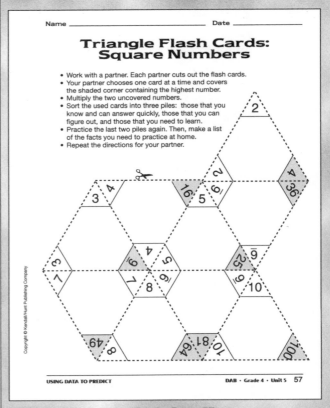

Name _____ Date _____

Triangle Flash Cards: Square Numbers

- Work with a partner. Each partner cuts out the flash cards.
- Your partner chooses one card at a time and covers the shaded corner containing the highest number.
- Multiply the two uncovered numbers.
- Sort the used cards into three piles: those that you know and can answer quickly, those that you can figure out, and those that you need to learn.
- Practice the last two piles again. Then, make a list of the facts you need to practice at home.
- Repeat the directions for your partner.

USING DATA TO PREDICT   DAB · Grade 4 · Unit 5   57

Discovery Assignment Book - Page 57

Part 5 Making Predictions from a Graph

The data below shows the winning times women swam the 200-meter backstroke at the Olympics. The winning times are given to the nearest second.

Time (in years)	Time (in seconds)
1968	145
1972	139
1976	133
1980	132
1984	132
1988	129
1992	127
1996	128
2000	128

1. Plot the data on a piece of *Centimeter Graph Paper*. Scale the vertical axis to 150 seconds. Scale the horizontal axis by fours, from 1960 to 2008. Then, answer Questions 2–7. Use a separate sheet of paper if you need to.

2. A. What variable did you plot on the horizontal axis on the graph? _____

   B. Is this variable numerical or categorical? _____

3. What variable did you plot on the vertical axis? _____

4. About how many minutes was the winning time for the 200-meter backstroke in 1992? _____

5. Do the points lie close to a line? _____ If they do, use a ruler to draw a best-fit line through the points.

6. Describe the graph. What does it tell you about the history of the 200-meter backstroke?

7. Can you use this graph to predict the winning time for the women's 200-meter backstroke in the year 2008? _____ If so, how? What is your prediction?

USING DATA TO PREDICT   DAB · Grade 4 · Unit 5   55

Discovery Assignment Book - Page 55

 **Journal Prompt**

The *Olympic Long Jump* graph tells a story. Write this story in words.

Extension

Students can look up the distance of winning long jumps on the web or in an Olympic record book and add any new data points to the graph on the *Olympic Long Jump* transparency. Is the pattern of points on the graph still the same? Has Bob Beamon's Olympic record been beaten? The class can also investigate the times and distances of other Olympic events by making graphs and looking for patterns.

Social Studies Connection

The graph of the Olympic long jump data is interesting historically. Note that there are no data points for the years 1916, 1940, and 1944 since there were no Olympics during World War I and World War II. After these years, the length of the jumps falls well below pre-war levels and then gradually increases again. The data point for 1936 represents Jesse Owens's jump in the 1936 Olympics in Nazi Germany prior to World War II. Note that the length of his jump was not surpassed until 1960. The story of Jessie Owens's participation in the 1936 Olympics can make for an interesting discussion.

Software Connection

Students can organize the data for other Olympic events in a spreadsheet or graphing program such as *Graph Master*. Many programs will produce a point graph and some will fit a line to the points.

AT A GLANCE

Math Facts and Daily Practice and Problems

DPP items A and B both practice math facts for square numbers. Item C reviews place value and base-ten shorthand. Item D provides practice with addition and subtraction.

Part 1. Predictions from Graphs

1. The class discusses patterns in two graphs on the *Predictions from Graphs* Activity Pages in the *Student Guide* and uses them to make predictions. Display the *Olympic Long Jump* and *Mile Run* Transparency Masters as you discuss the graphs.
2. The best-fit line is introduced in *Question 9.* Model drawing a best-fit line using the *Mile Run* Transparency Master.
3. Interpolation and extrapolation are introduced in *Question 12.*

Part 2. Using Best-Fit Lines

1. Students practice drawing best-fit lines and using them to make predictions on the *Using Best-Fit Lines* Activity Pages in the *Discovery Assignment Book.* Use the *Nila's Sit-Ups* Transparency Master to model drawing a best-fit line and using the line to make predictions. *(Question 1)*
2. Students complete *Questions 2–7.*

Homework

Assign Part 1 and Part 5 of the Home Practice.

Assessment

Use the *Observational Assessment Record* to record students' abilities to draw a best-fit line through a set of data points.

Notes:

Olympic Long Jump

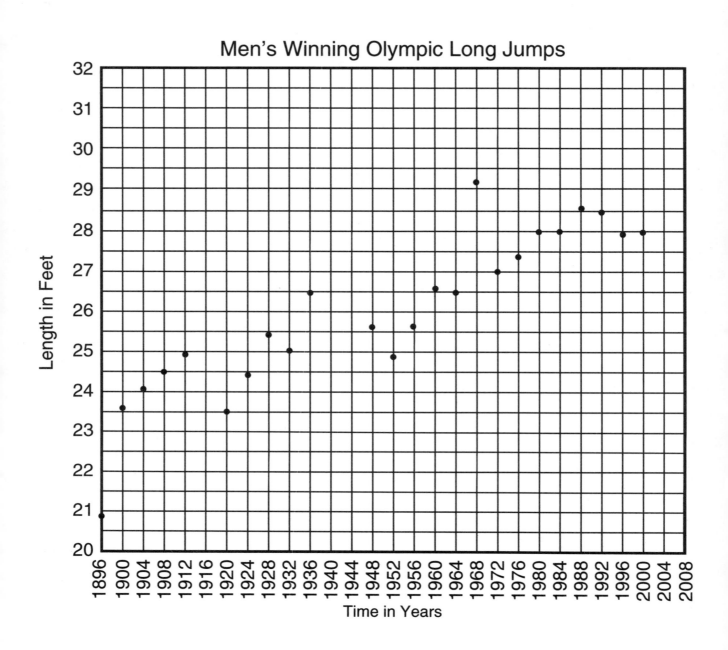

Men's Winning Olympic Long Jumps

Length in Feet (y-axis: 20 to 32)

Time in Years (x-axis: 1896 to 2008)

Mile Run

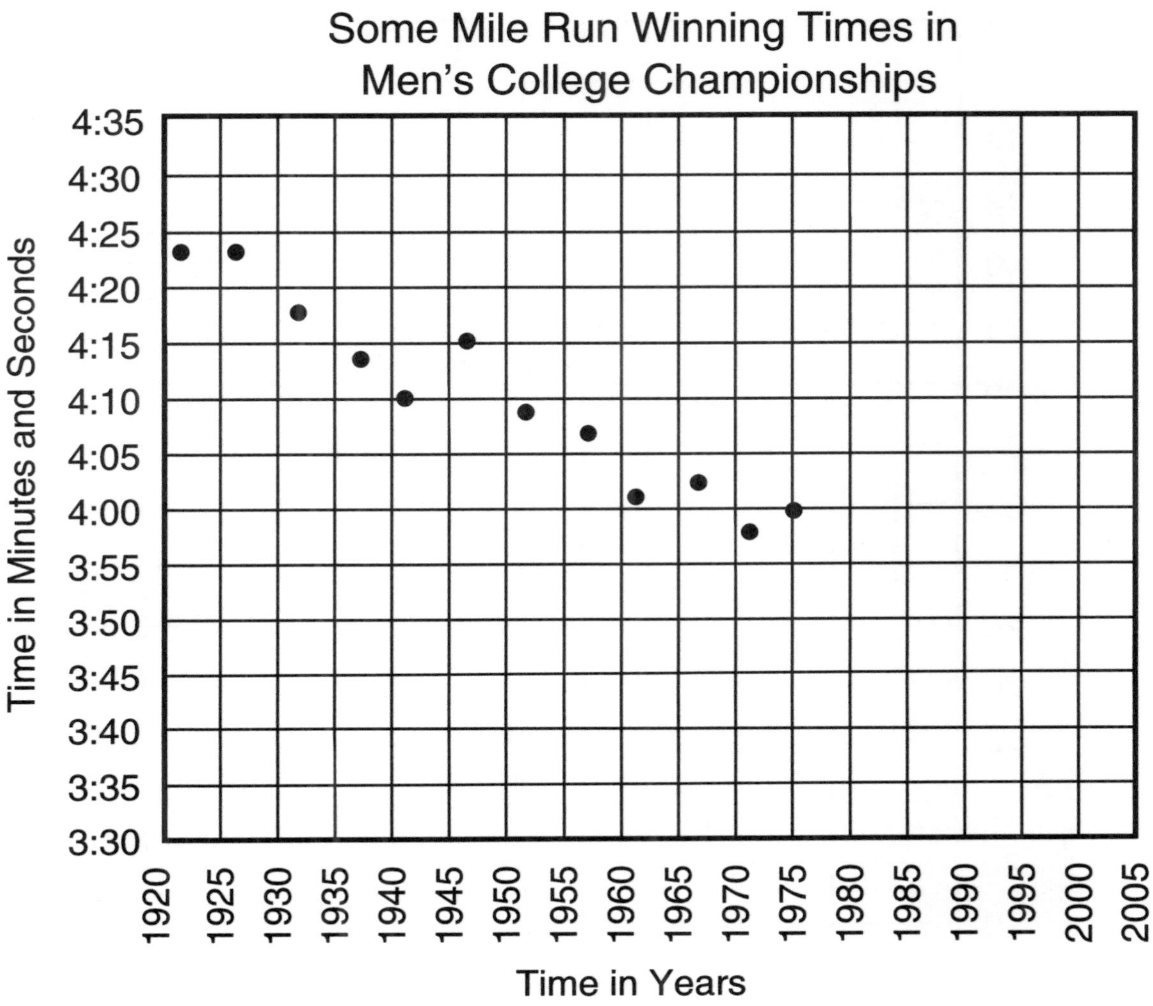
Some Mile Run Winning Times in Men's College Championships
Time in Minutes and Seconds
4:35
4:30
4:25
4:20
4:15
4:10
4:05
4:00
3:55
3:50
3:45
3:40
3:35
3:30
1920
1925
1930
1935
1940
1945
1950
1955
1960
1965
1970
1975
1980
1985
1990
1995
2000
2005
Time in Years

Nila's Sit-Ups

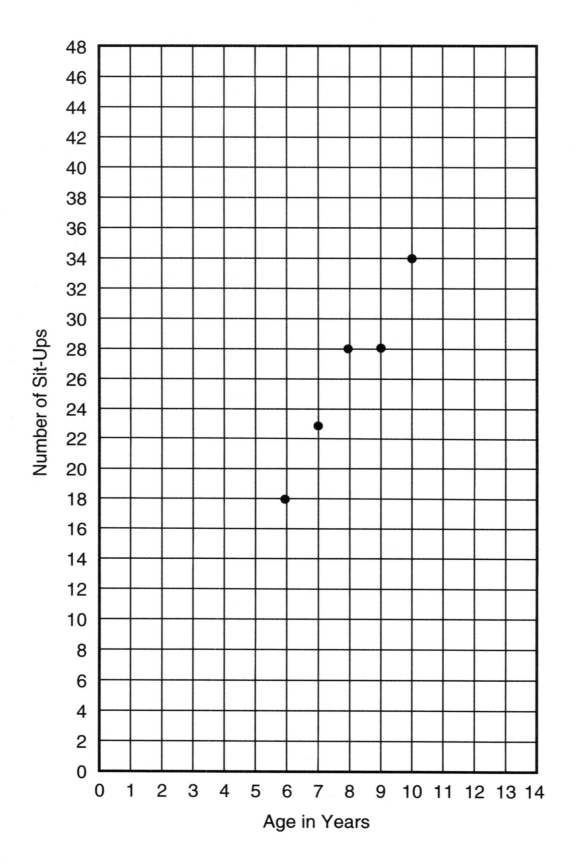

Student Guide

Questions 1–12 (SG pp. 120–124)

1. **A.** Time in years
   B. Length in feet
2. **A.** About $26\frac{1}{2}$ feet or 26 feet 6 inches
   B. Answers will vary.
   C. 24 years
3. *
4. **A.** *Approximately 29 feet 2 inches
   B. *
   C. *
5. **A.** Time in years
   B. Time in minutes and seconds
6. 4 minutes and 10 seconds
7. 1971
8. **A.** Answers will vary. The points form a "bumpy" line.
   B. downhill
   C. The winning time for running the mile decreased over the years.
9. **A.** *The line is drawn to fit the points as closely as possible.
   B. *3
   C. *5
   D. *4
10. *between 4 minutes and 5 seconds and 4 minutes and 10 seconds
11. *under 3 minutes and 45 seconds
12. **A.** *interpolation
    B. *extrapolation
    C. *

Discovery Assignment Book

**Home Practice (DAB p. 55)

Part 5. Making Predictions from a Graph

Questions 1–7

1.
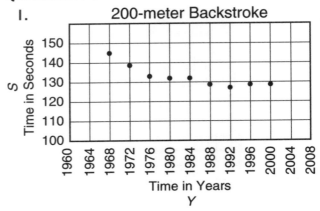

2. **A.** Time in Years
   B. Numerical
3. Time in Seconds
4. about 2 minutes
5. Yes.

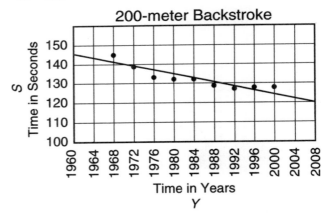

6. Answers will vary. Students might say that the times are decreasing, the graph is going downhill, or that women are getting to be faster swimmers.
7. Predictions will vary. About 121 seconds. Accept predictions between 115 and 125 seconds. Discuss that predictions beyond the data are not always reliable.

---

*Answers and/or discussion are included in the Lesson Guide.

**Answers for all the Home Practice in the *Discovery Assignment Book* are at the end of the unit.

Using Best-Fit Lines (DAB pp. 59–64)

Questions 1–7

*1. A. Answers will vary. Students may state that the points tend to go uphill or that Nila can do more and more sit-ups as she gets older.

B. uphill

C. Answers will vary. Nila can do more and more sit-ups as she gets older. She made no progress in the number of sit-ups she could do between the ages of 8 and 9.

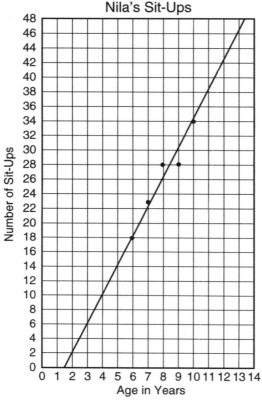

Nila's Sit-Ups

D. Yes

E. Predictions will vary. About 42. Accept predictions between 39 and 46 sit-ups.

F. Yes

2. A. Answers will vary. Students might say that John is becoming a faster runner or that the graph tends to go downhill.

B. downhill

C. Yes

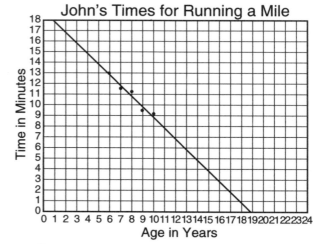

John's Times for Running a Mile

D. Predictions will vary. About 7 minutes.

E. *Predictions will vary. According to our graph, John will run the mile in about one minute. This is impossible. Students should see that extrapolating this far beyond the last data point is unreliable.

F. *Yes, but not for values far beyond the data points.

3. A. *Descriptions will vary. The points on the graph are scattered in no apparent order.

B. *No

C. *No

D. Students should see that they cannot make reliable predictions on the graph since there is no pattern.

---

*Answers and/or discussion are included in the Lesson Guide.

**Answers for all the Home Practice in the *Discovery Assignment Book* are at the end of the unit.

4. A. Descriptions will vary. The points on the graph go uphill and the more cookies you have, the more mass there is.

B. Yes, the points lie on a straight line.

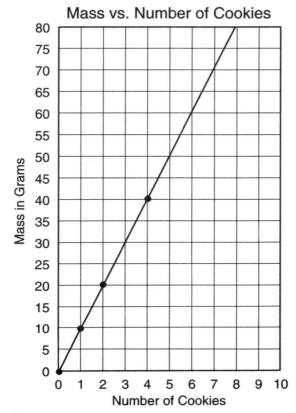

Mass vs. Number of Cookies

C. 30 grams

D. 50 grams

E. Interpolation

5. A. Descriptions will vary. The points tend to go uphill, but not in a line. They go uphill in a curve and level off.

B. The points lie on a curve, so it does not make sense to draw a best-fit line.

C. *Predictions will vary. About 42 cm. Accept predictions between 41 and 43 cm.

6. A. Descriptions will vary. The points tend to go downhill and as the years go by, women are becoming faster swimmers.

B.

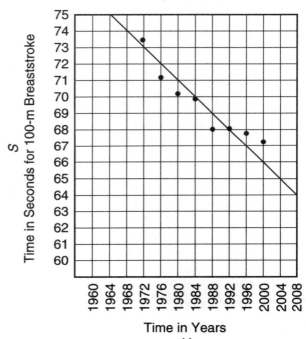

Winning Times for the Women's Olympic Breaststroke

7. The Mass vs. Number of Cookies graph. Its points lie on a straight line.

Daily Practice and Problems: Bit for Lesson 2

E. Finding Prime Factors

   (URG p. 11)

Write 90 as the product of prime numbers.

DPP Challenge is on page 42. Suggestions for using the DPPs are on page 42.

LESSON GUIDE

Another Average Activity

Estimated Class Sessions: 1–2

In this lesson, students investigate the meaning of averages by working with connecting cubes. By manipulating the cubes in towers of different heights, they find the median and mean of a set of data. The activity provides students with a visual image that will help them understand the procedures for finding the median and the mean. In Lesson 3, students will use calculators to compute the mean.

Key Content

- Investigating the concept of averages as a representative value for a data set.
- Averaging: finding the median and mean.
- Connecting mathematics to real-world situations.

Key Vocabulary

average
mean
median

Curriculum Sequence

Before This Unit

Averages. In third grade and Unit 1 of fourth grade, students used medians to average sets of data.

After This Unit

Averages. In this unit and succeeding units, students will use either means or medians to average data. See Units 10 and 13.

Materials List

Print Materials for Students

		Math Facts and Daily Practice and Problems	Activity	Homework
Student Book	**Student Guide**		*Another Average Activity* Pages 125–130	*Another Average Activity* Homework Section Pages 130–131
Teacher Resource	**Unit Resource Guide**	DPP Items E–F Pages 11–12 ⊙		

⊙ *available on Teacher Resource CD*

All Transparency Masters, Blackline Masters, and Assessment Blackline Masters in the Unit Resource Guide are on the Teacher Resource CD.

Supplies for Each Student Pair

80 connecting cubes or 120 square-inch tiles
small paper bag

Materials for the Teacher

Observational Assessment Record (Unit Resource Guide, Pages 7–8 and Teacher Resource CD)

Before the Activity

Before students begin the activity, fill each of the paper bags with about 80 separate connecting cubes.

This activity is described using connecting cubes. If your class does not have connecting cubes, borrow them from a primary teacher or substitute square-inch tiles for the cubes. Where the activity asks students to build towers, students can make rows of square-inch tiles on their desks as shown in Figure 2.

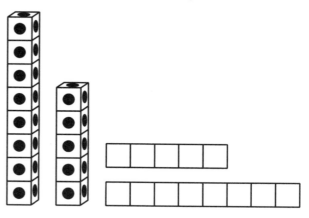

Figure 2: *Students can make towers of connecting cubes or rows of square-inch tiles.*

Developing the Activity

Part 1. Using Connecting Cubes to Explore Averages

Begin by asking students to read the first paragraph on the *Another Average Activity* Activity Pages in the *Student Guide.* On five spelling tests, Ming spells 7, 9, 7, 7, and 10 words correctly. When he averages his score by finding the median, he agrees that 7 words correct is his typical score. However, he thinks his scores of 9 and 10 should bring his grade up. Use *Questions 1–3* to discuss Ming's scores, review medians, and develop a context for learning to use the mean to find an average.

Have students build towers of cubes to represent Ming's five spelling tests. If possible, ask students to use one color for each tower. See Figure 3. The number of cubes in each tower corresponds to the number of correct words on each test. Students "even out" the five towers, moving cubes from the higher towers to the shorter ones. Ask:

- *What does each stack represent?* (One test score)
- *What does each cube represent?* (One word spelled correctly)

Another Average Activity

Every week the students in Room 204 take a spelling test of 10 words. Each student records the number of words he or she spells correctly in a table. Mrs. Dewey reports the average score to the parents.
Here are Ming's scores:

Ming's Scores

Test	Words Correct
Test #1	7
Test #2	9
Test #3	7
Test #4	7
Test #5	10

My median score is 7 words correct, so that is my average score. I guess you could say that 7 is a typical score, but it seems that the 9 and 10 should help bring my grades up.

 Discuss

1. **A.** Do you agree that 7 words correct is Ming's median score?
   B. How do you find the median of a set of numbers?

2. In Unit 1, you learned that an **average** is one number that represents a set of data. For this data, the median number of words correct is 7. Is 7 a good number to represent all of Ming's scores? Why or why not?

3. Averages can also be used to make predictions. Do you think 7 words correct is a good prediction for the typical score on Ming's next five spelling tests? Why or why not?

The **median** is a useful average because it is often easy to find. Since it is the number that is exactly in the middle of the data, it can be used to describe what is normal or typical for that data. However, we can also use another kind of average to represent a set of data. This average is called the **mean**.

Another Average Activity   SG · Grade 4 · Unit 5 · Lesson 2 125

Student Guide - Page 125

- *What happens when we "even" the stacks out?* (The cubes from the higher stacks fill in the shorter stacks, to make 8 cubes in each stack.)
- *Do we still have the same number of cubes?* (Yes)
- *Do we still have the same number of words spelled correctly?* (Yes)
- *How many total words did Ming spell correctly on his five tests?* (40)
- *If he had spelled the same number of words correctly on each test, how many cubes would be in each of the 5 stacks?* (8 cubes each)

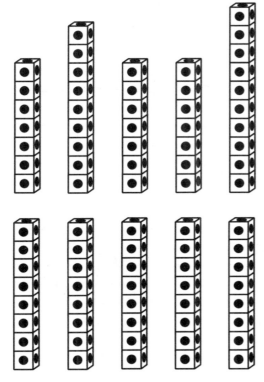

Figure 3: *Towers representing Ming's spelling scores (7, 9, 7, 7, and 10 words) and the towers evened out to show the mean of 8 words*

Question 4 asks if 8 is a good number to represent all of Ming's spelling scores. Although Ming never spelled 8 words correctly on any of the tests, 8 does fairly represent all of the scores. Ming spelled a total of 40 words correctly on all five tests, so if he spelled the same number of words correctly on all the tests, each of his scores would have been eight. Evening out the towers illustrates this point without using division to find the mean.

Question 5 asks how the scores of 9 and 10 affected the mean score. Taking the cubes from the towers with 9 and 10 cubes and placing them on the towers with 7 cubes increases the number of cubes in those towers to 8 cubes. This shows how the higher scores increase Ming's average.

Mrs. Dewey showed Ming how to use the mean to average his spelling scores. She used connecting cubes. She said, "Each cube represents one spelling word. Make a tower of cubes to represent each of your spelling test scores. For example, the first tower will have 7 cubes because you spelled 7 words correctly on that test."

After Ming made these five towers, Mrs. Dewey said, "Using just the cubes in your towers, even them out so that each of the five towers has the same number of cubes."

When the towers are evened out, the number of cubes in each of your towers is the mean.

Then my mean score is 8, and I can say that my average score is 8.

4. Is 8 a good number to represent all of Ming's scores? Why or why not?

5. How did the scores of 9 and 10 affect the mean score for Ming's tests?

126 SG · Grade 4 · Unit 5 · Lesson 2   **Another Average Activity**

Student Guide - Page 126

Content Note

Median or Mean? For many sets of data, the median and the mean will be very close to one another. In these cases, the choice of the mean or median may depend on how easy it is to do the calculations. The median is often easier to find, and for this reason, students have used it successfully to average data collected in labs in Grades 1, 2, and 3 and can continue to do so in Grade 4. We introduce the mean because, although it is harder to compute, it is the most commonly used average and it often represents the data better than the median.

When calculating the mean, every value is involved in the computation. Using Ming's spelling scores as an example, we find the **mean** by adding the scores and dividing by the number of scores: $(7 + 9 + 7 + 7 + 10) \div 5 = 8$. The scores of 9 and 10 pulled his average up. When finding the median, individual values are not taken into account. Ming's **median** score is 7 because it is the middle value when the scores are ranked in order from smallest to largest. The 9 and the 10 are not taken into account. (See the TIMS Tutor: *Averages* in the *Teacher Implementation Guide* for a more detailed explanation of the advantages and disadvantages of both the median and the mean and examples of situations when one is more appropriate to use than the other.)

Students do not need to master the subtleties of the differences between means and medians at this time. Our intent is to give students experience using both, so that they can use one or the other when they collect data for labs and activities.

Mrs. Dewey showed all the students in Room 204 how to find the median and the mean using connecting cubes. Students worked in pairs to complete the activity. Irma and Tanya's work is described on the following pages. Work with a partner to follow their example.

Irma and Tanya took turns pulling a handful of cubes from a paper bag and then building towers with the cubes. Together they made the five towers shown in the picture.

6. With your partner, build towers with the same numbers of cubes as in the picture.

Mrs. Dewey asked students to use one number, an average, to describe all of the towers. One way to do this is to find the median. To do this, the girls lined up their towers from shortest to tallest.

7. Line up your towers as shown in the picture.

8. The number of cubes in the middle tower is the median. What is the median number of cubes?

Another Average Activity   SG · Grade 4 · Unit 5 · Lesson 2   127

Student Guide - Page 127

To find the mean, the girls tried to "even out" the towers so that they all had the same number of cubes.

9. Even out your towers. (Hint: You can only use the cubes that are already in your towers and you must keep the same number of towers.)

10. Now each tower has about the same number of cubes. This number is the mean. What is the mean?

11. The median number of cubes in Tanya and Irma's towers was nine. Do you agree that nine cubes is a normal handful for Irma and Tanya? Why or why not?

12. The mean number of cubes in the girls' towers was ten. Do you agree that this number can also describe a normal handful? Why or why not?

13. Scientists use averages to make predictions. Predict the number of cubes Tanya or Irma would pull, if they pulled another handful.

14. With your partner, complete the same activity that Irma and Tanya did.
   A. Return the cubes to your bag. Be sure they have all been separated.
   B. Pull out one handful of cubes and build a tower with the cubes in your hand. Take turns with your partner until you have built five towers.
   C. Find the median number of cubes in your towers.
   D. Draw a picture of your towers. Record the median on your drawing.
   E. Find the mean number of cubes. Record the mean on your drawing. (Remember, you must keep the same number of towers. Do not add any more cubes from the bag or put any cubes back in the bag.)

128 SG · Grade 4 · Unit 5 · Lesson 2   Another Average Activity

Student Guide - Page 128

The Explore section on the *Another Average Activity* Activity Pages describes the actions of two students, Tanya and Irma, as they complete an activity with connecting cubes. Have pairs of students in your class imitate the actions of the two girls described on these pages. They should build towers with the same number of cubes as shown in the illustrations.

Students find the median by lining up the towers from shortest to tallest as described in *Questions 6–8*. *Questions 9–10* guide students through finding the mean with the towers of cubes. They remove individual cubes from the taller towers and place them on the shorter towers until all the towers have about the same number of cubes. Ask:

- *How many cubes are now in each tower?* (Four towers have 10 cubes and one tower has 9 cubes.)
- *Can we make all the towers exactly even?* (No)
- *However, each tower has about the same number of cubes. This number is the mean. Which number, 9 or 10, is the best choice for the mean? Why?* (10, because there are more towers with 10 cubes than there are with 9 cubes.)

Ten cubes approximates the mean since most of the towers had 10 cubes. This is equivalent to rounding the mean to the nearest whole number. *Questions 11–12* draw attention to both the median and the mean as reasonable representative numbers for Tanya and Irma's handfuls of cubes. *Question 13* points out the uses of averages to make predictions.

> **TIMS Tip**
> The class may need to define "handful" since children often think bigger is better. Guidelines similar to the following may be helpful: Grab the cubes with one hand without touching the bag with the other hand; and shake your hand gently before taking it out of the bag.

Question 14 instructs students to repeat the same activity as Tanya and Irma. They pull handfuls of cubes out of a paper bag and build a tower with each handful. Each pair of students makes a total of five towers. Remind students to build each tower with just the cubes from one handful and not to supplement with more cubes from the bag. To find the **median** number of cubes in a tower, students line up the towers from smallest to largest. The number of cubes in the middle tower is the median. To find the **mean,** they "even out" the towers until each tower has about the same number of cubes. The mean is the number of cubes in each tower after the cubes have been rearranged. Ask:

- *If you were to tell a friend about how many cubes you could pull in one handful, what number would you use?* (Answers vary.)

- *Why did you choose this number? Is this number your mean or your median?*

- *Is an average a good number to use to describe a normal handful?* (Yes)

Part 2. Using Cubes to Solve Problems

In this part of the activity, students will use connecting cubes to answer *Questions 15–21. Question 15* asks for the median and mean number of people in five households. As students build the five towers, ask:

- *What does each tower represent?* (A household)

- *What does each cube represent?* (A person in the household)

When they find the median and the mean, remind the class that both the averages can be used to represent a typical household on Jacob's block.

Question 16 asks students to find the median and mean of four quiz scores. Finding the median of an even number of scores will be a new problem since there is no score that is the middle. In this case there are two middle towers—one with seven cubes and one with eight cubes. Since $7\frac{1}{2}$ is exactly halfway between the two, $7\frac{1}{2}$ is the median. See the discussion in Lesson 3 of Unit 1.

To find the mean number of scores, students will again "even out" the towers. In this case they will have three towers of seven cubes each and one tower of eight cubes. Ask:

- *How can we decide what is the mean? 7 or 8? Why?* (7 problems, because there are more towers with 7 cubes)

Question 17 may seem tricky to students, since all the numbers to be averaged are the same. However, if they understand that an average is one number that can be used to describe a set of numbers, then they will see that the median and mean age of five ten-year-olds is ten. If students are skeptical, have them build the 5 towers of ten each and line them up.

Questions 18–20 ask students to compare the median to the mean. The median and the mean are alike because they both tell us what is typical for a given situation *(Question 18)*. The mean is found by "evening out" the numbers in the data set, and the median is

Using Cubes to Solve Problems
Solve the following problems. Use towers of cubes to help you.

15. Jacob surveyed five families on his block. He filled in the following data table. Jacob found the median and the mean number of people in a household using towers.

    A. Jacob built five towers. Why?
    B. What did each tower stand for?
    C. What did each cube stand for?
    D. Use towers to find the median.
    E. Use towers to find the mean.
       (*Hint:* Use the closest number for your answer.)

Jacob's Data

Family	Number of People in Household
Scott-Haines	2
Thomas	6
Molina	3
Chang	5
Green	3

16. When Mrs. Dewey was in the fourth grade, she took a math quiz each week. Every quiz had ten problems. She got 10 problems right the first week, 7 problems right the second week, 8 problems right the third week, and 4 problems right the fourth week. Use towers to find the median and mean.

    A. How many towers will you build?
    B. What does each tower stand for?
    C. What does each cube stand for?
    D. Find the median. (*Hint:* What number is halfway between the number of cubes in the middle two towers?)
    E. Even out the towers to find the mean. (You must use the same number of towers as in 16A.)

17. When Rita, a new Girl Scout leader, was introduced to her group of girls, she asked them how old they were. Keenya, Shannon, Ana, Grace, and Maya all said they were 10 years old.

    A. What one number can be used to describe the age of the girls?
    B. What is the median age for this group of Girl Scouts?
    C. What is the mean?

18. How are the two kinds of averages alike? (*Hint:* What do they tell us?)

19. How are the mean and the median different? (*Hint:* How do you find each one?)

Another Average Activity   SG · Grade 4 · Unit 5 · Lesson 2 129

Student Guide - Page 129

found by finding the number in the middle of the data *(Question 19)*. The median is often the easiest to find because it is simply a matter of lining up the data values from smallest to largest and choosing the middle value *(Question 20)*.

For *Questions 21A–21B* students again use cubes to find the mean and median of three distances a car rolls: 13 cm, 14 cm, and 18 cm. *Question 21C* asks students which of the two averages better describes the distances. Reasonable arguments can be made for both the median and the mean. Since the shorter two distances are much closer together than the third distance, the median (14 cm) may be a better predictor of the distance the car will roll on a fourth try. However, the mean (15 cm) takes the 18 cm roll into account.

Suggestions for Teaching the Lesson

Homework and Practice

- Assign the Homework section in the *Student Guide.* Students use towers of pennies or small building blocks to find medians and means.

- DPP Bit E asks students to find the prime factorization of 90. Challenge F presents a problem in which students calculate how long to cook a 20 pound turkey.

<table>
<tr><td colspan="2">20. Which average is easier to find?</td></tr>
<tr><td>21.</td><td>Roberto rolled a toy car down a ramp and measured the distance it rolled. The first time it rolled 13 cm; the second time it rolled 14 cm; and the third time it rolled 18 cm.</td></tr>
<tr><td></td><td>A. Find the median distance the car rolled.</td></tr>
<tr><td></td><td>B. Find the mean.</td></tr>
<tr><td></td><td>C. Which number, the mean or the median, better describes the distance the car rolls? Explain your answer.</td></tr>
</table>

Homework

Dear Family Member:

In class, students used towers of cubes to learn how to find two kinds of averages: the mean and the median. You can look back at the previous pages in this section to see how this is done. In the next lesson, students will learn how to compute an average using calculators.

Use pennies or small building blocks to build towers to solve the following problems. You will need about 30 pennies or blocks.

1. Linda counted the number of plants her mom has in each room in the house. She filled in the following data table.
   A. Find the median number of plants in the house.
   B. Find the mean.

Linda's Data

Room	Number of Plants
Kitchen	5
Living Room	8
Family Room	7
Linda's Room	1
Bathroom	2
Dining Room	2
Mom's Room	3

Another Average Activity

Student Guide - Page 130

(URG p. 12)

Daily Practice and Problems: Challenge for Lesson 2

F. Challenge: Cooking a Turkey

Roberto's mother put a turkey in the oven at 11:30. The instructions say that the turkey should cook about 17 minutes per pound. The turkey weighs 20 pounds.

1. About how long should Roberto's mother cook the turkey?

2. About what time will the turkey be ready?

3. Roberto's mother decided that the turkey was ready at 5:20. How long did the turkey cook?

Assessment

- *Question 3* in the Homework section can be used as an assessment item. Ask students to write their answers and explanations.

- Use the *Observational Assessment Record* to note students' abilities to find medians and means by manipulating connecting cubes.

Extension

Tell the class that each student will pull one handful of cubes from a bag or bucket and build a tower. Ask them to predict the average number of cubes that will be pulled. Let each student grab a handful and build a tower. Find the median number of cubes in a tower by lining up all the towers and choosing the middle tower. Find the mean by evening out the towers. Discuss the results. Did students make good predictions?

---

2. John wanted to see how many free-throws he could make in one minute. The first minute he made 6 baskets. The second minute he made only 3. The third minute he made 6 baskets again. The fourth minute he made 9.
   A. Find the median number of baskets.
   B. Find the mean.

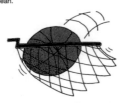

3. The students in Mrs. Dewey's class record the number of books they read each week. Here is Jerome's data.

Jerome's Data

Week	Number of Books
Week #1	3
Week #2	2
Week #3	5
Week #4	2
Week #5	2

A. Find the median.
B. Use towers to find the mean. Give your answer to the nearest whole book.
C. Which average (the median or the mean) do you think better represents the number of books that Jerome read? Why?

Another Average Activity   SG · Grade 4 · Unit 5 · Lesson 2 131

Student Guide - Page 131

AT A GLANCE

Math Facts and Daily Practice and Problems

DPP Bit E reviews prime factors. Challenge F asks students to calculate time.

Part 1. Using Connecting Cubes to Explore Averages

1. Students read the opening paragraph on the *Another Average Activity* Activity Pages in the *Student Guide*.
2. Use *Questions 1–5* to guide a discussion that reviews medians and introduces means.
3. In *Questions 6–14,* pairs of students use connecting cubes to model procedures for finding medians and means. They find the median and mean number of cubes in five handfuls of cubes drawn from a paper bag.

Part 2. Using Cubes to Solve Problems

In *Questions 15–21* students work together to solve problems involving medians and means using the cubes.

Homework

Assign the Homework section in the *Student Guide*.

Assessment

1. Use *Question 3* in the Homework section as an assessment.
2. Use the *Observational Assessment Record* to note students' abilities to find medians and means using connecting cubes.

Notes:

Student Guide

Questions 1–21 (SG pp. 125–130)

1. **A.** Yes. Arrange the numbers from smallest to largest: 7, 7, 7, 9, 10—7 is in the middle.

    B. List the numbers in order and find the middle value.

2. Answers will vary. Students should be able to justify their answers. One possible response: No, Ming scored higher than a 7 on two tests. The 9 and 10 should bring his grade up. Another possible response: Yes. He scored 7 three times and 7 is the median.

3. Answers will vary but students must justify their answers. No, the 9 and 10 in the data shows that Ming could do better than a 7. Or, Yes. 7 is the median score and you can use it to make predictions. See the Content Note in Lesson Guide 2.

4. *

5. *

6.–7. Students should build five towers and line them up in order as shown in the *Student Guide.*

8. 9 cubes

9. See the figure in the *Student Guide.*

10. *10 cubes

11. Yes; 9 is the median. Tanya and Irma pulled handfuls smaller than 9 and larger than 9. The middle value is a good predictor.

12. Yes; 10 is the mean. Taking the cubes from the towers with 11 and 13 cubes and placing them on the towers with 7 and 9 cubes increased the number of cubes in those towers to 10 cubes. The higher values, 11 cubes and 13 cubes, increase the average. The mean (10 cubes) is the number of cubes the girls would have pulled, if they pulled the same number each time. See the Content Note in Lesson Guide 2.

13. 9 or 10 cubes

14. *Answers will vary.

15. **A.** He surveyed five families.

    B. Each tower stands for one family.

    C. Each cube stands for one family member.

    D. 3 people

    E. 4 people; When evening out towers, students should end up with 4 towers of 4 cubes and 1 tower of 3 cubes. Since most of the towers have 4 cubes, the mean is 4.

16. **A.** 4 towers

    B. Each tower stands for one math quiz score.

    C. Each cube represents a correct answer.

    D. *$7\frac{1}{2}$ correct problems

    E. *7 correct problems

17. **A.** *10 years old

    B. *10 years

    C. *10 years

18. *

19. *

20. *

21. **A.** 14 cm

    B. 15 cm

    C. *

Homework (SG pp. 130–131)

Questions 1–3

1. **A.** 3 plants

    B. 4 plants

2. **A.** 6 baskets

    B. 6 baskets

3. **A.** 2 books

    B. 3 books

    C. Answers will vary. The higher values, 3 and 5, are involved in the computation of the mean and therefore increase the average to 3 books. The median (2) does not take into account the week Jerome read 3 books nor the week he read 5 books; however, it is a "typical" number of books that Jerome read during the 5-week period.

*Answers and/or discussion are included in the Lesson Guide.

**Answers for all the Home Practice in the *Discovery Assignment Book* are at the end of the unit.

Daily Practice and Problems: Bits for Lesson 3

6. Using Exponents (URG p. 12)

A. $2^2 = ?$ B. $3^2 = ?$

C. $2^2 + 3^2 = ?$ D. $4^2 = ?$

E. $3^2 \times 5 = ?$ F. $2 \times 4^2 = ?$

I. Fact Families for the Square Numbers
(URG p. 13)

The square numbers have only two facts in each fact family.

For example, the following two facts are in the same fact family.

$$2 \times 2 = 4 \text{ and } 4 \div 2 = 2$$

Solve the fact given. Then, name the second fact that is in the same fact family.

1. $9 \times 9 = $ ___   2. $5 \times 5 = $ ___

3. $7 \times 7 = $ ___   4. $8 \times 8 = $ ___

5. $10 \times 10 = $ ___   6. $3 \times 3 = $ ___

7. $6 \times 6 = $ ___   8. $4 \times 4 = $ ___

9. $1 \times 1 = $ ___

DPP Tasks are on page 51. Suggestions for using the DPPs are on page 51.

LESSON GUIDE 3

The Meaning of the Mean

Estimated Class Sessions: 2–3

In the first part of the activity, students use strips of adding machine tape to model the process of finding the mean of a set of data through measurement. In the second part, they learn to find the mean on a calculator by summing the data and dividing by the number of data points. Students then practice finding means and medians. An assessment page is included with the activity.

Key Content

- Investigating the concept of averages as a representative value for a data set.

- Averaging: finding the mean.

Key Vocabulary

circumference
mean

Materials List

Print Materials for Students

	Math Facts and Daily Practice and Problems	Activity	Homework	Written Assessment
Student Book — Student Guide		*The Meaning of the Mean* Pages 132–137 and Student Rubric: *Telling* Appendix C and Inside Back Cover 🔘	*The Meaning of the Mean* Homework Section Page 138	
Teacher Resources — Facts Resource Guide 🔘	DPP Items 5G–5J			
Teacher Resources — Unit Resource Guide	DPP Items G–J Pages 12–13 🔘			*Cookie Factory* Page 54, 1 per student
Teacher Resources — Generic Section 🔘		*Two-column Data Table*, 1 per student		

🔘 *available on Teacher Resource CD*

All Transparency Masters, Blackline Masters, and Assessment Blackline Masters in the Unit Resource Guide are on the Teacher Resource CD.

Supplies for Each Student Group

roll of adding machine tape or ball of string
meterstick
scissors
adhesive tape
calculator
ruler
crayon

Materials for the Teacher

Transparency of Student Rubric: *Telling* (Teacher Implementation Guide, Assessment section)
Transparency of *Two-column Data Table* (Unit Resource Guide, Generic Section) or easel paper
   for class data paper

The Meaning of the Mean

The students in Mrs. Dewey's class are preparing for the Bessie Coleman School Olympic Day. The class wants to wear sweatbands around their heads during the races. To order the headbands, they need to know the average head circumference of the students in the class.

The class first worked together in groups of four students. They measured the distance around each person's head. Then, they found the mean circumference for each group.

Finding the Mean Circumference

Work with a group of four people to complete the same activity:

Measure head circumference with strips of paper:

- For each member of the group, wrap adding machine tape around the student's head.
- Mark the distance around the head with a crayon.
- Cut the adding machine tape at the crayon mark to make a strip that is the same length as the circumference of the student's head.
- Check the strip. Wrap it around the student's head again. The ends of the strip should just touch each other.

The Meaning of the Mean

Student Guide - Page 132

- Measure to the nearest centimeter.
- Make a data table like the one shown.

Group 1's Data

Name	Circumference of Head (in cm)
Michael	52 cm
Ming	56 cm
Shannon	50 cm
Roberto	54 cm

Even out the strips to find the mean:

- Tape the four strips together end-to-end to make one long strip. Be careful not to let the strips overlap.

No overlap!

- Fold the long strip into four equal parts. (Fold strip in half, then in half again.)

- Measure the length of one-fourth of the long strip to the nearest centimeter. This length is the mean.
- Write the mean for your group at the bottom of your data table.

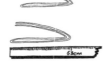

53 cm

When the students in Group 1 finished "evening out" the length of their strips, they found that one-fourth of the long strip measured 53 cm. This is the mean length of their strips. They reported to the class that on average the circumference of their heads is 53 cm.

The Meaning of the Mean

Student Guide - Page 133

Before the Activity

To decrease time students need to measure and cut the tape, tear strips of adding machine tape that are about 60 cm. Groups can then cut the strips the same lengths as each student's head circumference.

TIMS Tip

Since string stretches, measurements with string may not be as reliable. For this reason, adding machine tape is preferable if available.

Developing the Activity

Part 1. Finding the Mean Circumference Using Adding Machine Tape

Students begin the activity by reading *The Meaning of the Mean* Activity Pages in the *Student Guide* and following the directions. Groups measure the head circumference of each member using adding machine tape or string and record the measurements in a data table for the group. For each student, a strip of adding machine tape is cut the same length as his or her head circumference.

To find the average head circumference, each group tapes the strips together, taking care not to let the ends overlap. Then, the group folds this long strip into as many equal parts as there are students in the group. The length of each of these parts is the mean head circumference for the group. Each group should record the mean circumference at the bottom of their data table. Since it is easy to fold the strip into fourths, four students per group is a good choice.

TIMS Tip

If the number of students in your class is not divisible by four, then form as many groups of four as you can. The remaining groups can be groups of three. You may need to help these groups fold their long strip into three equal parts.

This process of taping the strips together and then folding the long strip in equal parts models the procedure for finding the mean. In the previous activity students "evened out" the heights of the towers of connecting cubes. Here the students "even out" the length of the strips. To find the mean numerically, we add up the values and divide by the number of values. This is similar to taping the strips together and then folding the strip into equal parts.

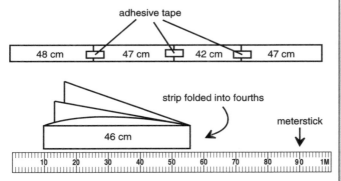

Figure 4: *Procedure for finding the mean using adhesive machine tape*

Discussing **Questions 1–3** on *The Meaning of the Mean* Activity Pages in the *Student Guide* will give you an opportunity to check students' understanding of the meaning of the mean. Each group should add their group's mean to a class data table. See Figure 5. These questions ask students to estimate the mean circumference for the entire class using the group means. During one class discussion, a student said that the mean should be a number "in the middle," not at the ends. This showed a good understanding of the concept.

Group	Mean Head Circumference
Michael's Group	53 cm
Jacob's Group	57 cm

Figure 5: *Sample data table of groups' means*

Part 2. Using a Calculator to Find the Mean
Questions 4–5 lead students toward developing a procedure for finding means using a calculator. These steps are explained in the Using a Calculator to Find the Mean section of *The Meaning of the Mean* Activity Pages.

Discuss

1. Report to the class the average circumference of the heads of the students in your group. Give the mean.
2. Compare the means for all the groups. What can you say about them?
3. Estimate the average circumference for the whole class using the means for each group.
4. **A.** How would you find the mean if there were five people in your group?
   B. Three people?
5. How could you use a calculator to find the mean? (*Hint:* What steps did you go through to find the mean using the strips?)

Explore

Using a Calculator to Find the Mean
Michael's group used a chart to think through its answer to Question 5.

Finding the Mean

Steps with adding machine tape	Steps on the calculator
1. We taped the strips together.	1. Add the lengths of the strips together. 56 + 52 + 50 + 54 = 212 cm
2. We folded the long strip into 4 equal parts.	2. Divide the total length by the number of people in our group. 212 + 4 = 53 cm
3. The length of one-fourth of the long strip is 53 cm.	3. The mean is 53 cm. On average, the circumference of our heads is 53 cm.

The Meaning of the Mean

Student Guide - Page 134

These are the keystrokes that Michael's group used. Try them on your calculator.

> What is showing on your display now? What does the number in the window tell you?

> What is showing on your display now? What does the number in the window tell you?

| 56 | + | 52 | + | 50 | + | 54 | = | + | 4 | = |

Michael's group found the mean by adding the values for each head circumference and dividing by the number of students in the group. The **mean** for any data set is an average that is found by adding the values in the set of data and dividing by the number of values.

6. The data for Group 2 is shown below.

Group 2's Data

Name	Circumference of Head (in cm)
Jacob	60 cm
Tanya	57 cm
Maya	56 cm
Jessie	54 cm

They used a calculator to find the mean for their data. The display on their calculator read 56.75.

Student Guide - Page 135

A. Write calculator keystrokes for finding the mean for Group 2.
B. Is 56.75 cm closer to 56 cm or 57 cm?

56.75 cm

C. Give the mean to the nearest whole centimeter.

7. A. Use your data table and your calculator to find the mean circumference for your group. Give your answer to the nearest centimeter. (*Hint:* Use a meterstick to help you find the nearest centimeter.)
   B. Compare the number you found on your calculator for the mean to the number your group found by measuring the folded strip. Are the numbers close?

8. Groups 3 and 4 only had three students.
   A. Find the mean for each data set. Give your answer to the nearest centimeter.
   B. Show the calculator keystrokes you used for finding the mean.
   C. Find the median for each set of data.

Group 3's Data		**Group 4's Data**	
Name	Circumference of Head (in cm)	Name	Circumference of Head (in cm)
John	58 cm	Keenya	53 cm
Jerome	59 cm	Grace	53 cm
Roberto	54 cm	Ana	51 cm

Student Guide - Page 136

As students try the calculator strokes in the example, show them how to use the clear entry key on their calculators. (This key is often labeled CE/C.) If students make a mistake entering data, they can correct the last entry by pushing the clear entry key and then entering the correct data. By using this key, they will not have to reenter all of the data if they make a mistake adding many numbers.

When students use the calculator to find means, decimal answers are inevitable. Since the measurements were recorded to the nearest centimeter, the means should be given to the nearest centimeter as well. *Question 6* is designed to help students do this. *Question 6A* asks students to give calculator strokes for finding the mean of 60 cm, 57 cm, 56 cm, and 54 cm. This may be the first time students have recorded the strokes, so you may need to model this for them. They can use the strokes shown in the *Student Guide* as an example. Then, *Question 6B* asks if the number on the display, 56.75, is closer to 56 cm or 57 cm. One way students can decide is by locating 56.75 cm on a meterstick and finding that 56.75 cm is closer to 57 cm. Another method is to ask them if $56.75 is closer to $56 or $57.

Question 7 asks each group to find the mean head circumference for the group using their data table and a calculator. Then, the group compares this answer to the number they found for the mean when they measured the folded strip. These numbers should be within one or two centimeters. If a group adds the numbers, but does not divide by the number of students in the group, remind them of our definition of an average: a number that will represent what is normal or typical for the group. Demonstrate by holding a group's long strip as if it were going around a giant's head. Ask:

- *This is four strips added together. Would this be a normal circumference for a fourth-grader?*
- *What should we do after we add?*

Questions 8–11 provide practice in finding means with a calculator and finding medians without using towers of cubes. *Question 11* asks students to find the average spelling score for a set of five scores: 13, 19, 12, 20, and 11 words correct. Students must choose to use the mean or the median. The median number of words correct is 13. The mean number of words correct is 15. One advantage of using the median is that it is often easier to find. The mean score is higher in this case because the computation involves the two higher scores. Students will probably feel that a score of 15 represents the scores better than a score of 13.

TIMS Tip

Students can work individually or in groups to answer *Questions 8–11.* To help students work effectively in groups, each member of a group can be assigned a role or a job. The following roles are appropriate for solving problems: *reader, checker, question commander,* and *materials monitor.* The reader reads the problem to the group. It is the checker's job to be sure that each member of the group understands the group's answer to a question or has written down a response before the reader reads the next question. The materials monitor collects needed materials, puts them away, and makes sure the group cleans up. The question commander is the only member of the group who can ask the teacher a question. If someone in the group has a question, the question commander refers the question to the other members of the group. The group must try to find an answer to the question. If they cannot, then the question commander may ask the teacher to answer the group's question.

Suggestions for Teaching the Lesson

Math Facts

DPP Bit G provides practice with math facts for the square numbers using exponents. Task H is a riddle that reviews square numbers under 100. Bit I provides practice through the use of fact families. Task J is a set of word problems that practice computation skills.

Homework and Practice

Assign the Homework section on *The Meaning of the Mean* Activity Pages in the *Student Guide.* Students will need a calculator to complete the homework.

---

9. Each day for a week, students in Room 204 recorded the temperature outside at noon.
   A. Find the mean temperature. Show your calculator keystrokes. Give your answer to the nearest whole degree.
   B. Find the median temperature.

Temperature Data

Day	Temperature at Noon in °F
Monday	47°
Tuesday	38°
Wednesday	37°
Thursday	43°
Friday	46°

10. In the first six soccer games of the season, Jackie's team scored 2, 3, 4, 0, 1, and 2 goals.
    A. Find the mean number of goals.
    B. Find the median number of goals.
    C. Look back. Do your answers make sense? Are the averages you found typical scores for Jackie's team?

11. Each week a fourth grade class has a test on 20 spelling words. A student got 13 right the first week, 19 right the second week, 12 right the third week, 20 right the fourth week, and 11 right the fifth week.
    A. On average, how many words did the student get right?
    B. Did you use the median or the mean? Why?

The Meaning of the Mean SG · Grade 4 · Unit 5 · Lesson 3 137

Student Guide - Page 137

Daily Practice and Problems:
Tasks for Lesson 3

H. Task: Number Puzzle (URG p. 12)

I am a square number less than 100.

I am a multiple of 2, but I am not a multiple of 8.

2 is not my only prime factor.

What number am I?

Explain your strategy.

J. Task: Grocery Shopping
(URG p. 13)

1. Paper towels cost 70¢ a roll. How much will 7 rolls cost?

2. Turkey sandwiches cost $2.50. How much will 3 sandwiches cost?

3. Frozen yogurt cups cost 59¢ apiece. About how much will 6 cups cost?

4. A juice pack has 3 juice boxes. A juice pack costs $0.90. How much is each juice box worth?

Homework

You will need a calculator to complete this homework.

1. The data table for a group of students from the experiment *Arm Span vs. Height* is shown below.

   A. Find the mean arm span for Jerome's group to the nearest inch. Show your calculator keystrokes.

   B. Find the median arm span.

   C. Find the mean height to the nearest inch.

   D. Find the median height.

   E. Look back at your answers. Do they make sense? Are they typical arm spans and heights for fourth graders?

Jerome's Group

Name	S Arm Span (in inches)	H Height (in inches)
Jerome	49	50
Keenya	54	55
Frank	59	57
Luis	58	58
Roberto	55	57

2. The students in Room 204 collected data on the number of times students have moved. Here is the data that one group collected: Shannon has moved 7 times, Linda has moved 3 times, Grace has moved 0 times, and Romesh has moved 2 times. Shannon said, "The average number of times we have moved is 12 times." Is Shannon correct? Why or why not?

3. John, Jackie, Nicholas, Irma, Maya, and Michael all walk to school together.

   John lives 1 block from school.
   Nicholas lives 2 blocks from school.
   Maya lives 4 blocks from school.

   Jackie lives 1 block from school.
   Irma lives 2 blocks from school.
   Michael lives 8 blocks from school.

   A. Find the median number of blocks the students live from school.

   B. Find the mean number of blocks.

   C. Michael lives much farther away from school than the other children. How does that affect the mean?

The Meaning of the Mean

Student Guide - Page 138

Student Rubric: Telling

In My Best Work in Mathematics:

- I show all of the steps that I used to solve the problem. I also tell what each number refers to (such as 15 boys or 6 inches).

- I explain why I solved the problem the way I did so that someone can see why my method makes sense.

- If I use tools like pictures, tables, graphs, or number sentences, I explain how the tools I used fit the problem.

- I use math words and symbols correctly. For example, if I see "6 – 2," I solve the problem "six minus two," not "two minus six."

Student Guide - Appendix C

Suggestions for Teaching the Lesson (*continued*)

Assessment

Use the *Cookie Factory* Assessment Blackline Master to assess students' skills in finding the median and mean of a set of numbers and their understanding of averages. *Question 2* asks students to find the mean and median number of chocolate chips in five cookies that have 10, 11, 5, 12, and 2 chips. They find that the mean number of chips is 8 and the median number of chips is 10. The factory claims that the average number of chips in its cookies is 10. *Question 2C* asks if students think the factory's claim is true. Since the median is an average, the factory's claim is true. However, students may feel that the mean represents all of the numbers in the data better than the median, since the cookies with 5 and 2 chips should pull the average down. You can encourage students to write a full explanation of their answers to *Question 2* by reviewing the Student Rubric: *Telling* which was introduced in Unit 2 Lesson 1.

> ### Journal Prompt
> John said, "The average family on my block has two pets." What do you think he means?

Software Connection

Students can enter their data for head circumference into a spreadsheet. They can then use the data to find the mean circumference. Many spreadsheet programs will also find medians as well.

AT A GLANCE

Math Facts and Daily Practice and Problems

DPP items G–J provide practice with the math facts for the square numbers through a variety of activities.

Part 1. Finding the Mean Circumference Using Adding Machine Tape

1. In *The Meaning of the Mean* Activity Pages in the *Student Guide,* students cut strips of adding machine tape the same length as the circumference of their heads. Working in groups of four, they tape the four strips together and fold this long strip into fourths. The length of one-fourth of the long strip is the mean.

2. In *Questions 1–3,* groups report the mean circumference for their group to the class and record it in a class data table. They use this data to estimate the average head circumference of the students in the class.

3. *Questions 4–5* lead students toward developing a procedure for finding the mean using a calculator.

Part 2. Using a Calculator to Find the Mean

1. This section of *The Meaning of the Mean* Activity Pages introduces the use of calculators to find the mean.

2. *Questions 6–7* ask students to find the mean circumference for their group using a calculator.

3. *Questions 8–11* provide practice in finding means and medians.

Homework

Assign the Homework section. Students will need calculators to complete the assignment.

Assessment

Students complete the *Cookie Factory* Assessment Blackline Master.

Notes:

Cookie Factory

You may use a calculator or connecting cubes to help you solve the following problems.

1. At a cookie factory, a worker finds the mass of 4 cookies. The mass of the cookies is 11 grams, 6 grams, 11 grams, and 9 grams.

   A. Find the median mass of the cookies.

   B. Find the mean.

2. A chocolate chip cookie factory claims that the cookies from the factory have an average of 10 chocolate chips in a cookie. When a worker inspected 5 cookies, she found the following number of chips: 10, 11, 5, 12, and 2.

   A. Find the median number of chips.

   B. Find the mean number of chips.

   C. Do you think the factory's claim is true? Why or why not? Write a clear explanation of your answer.

Student Guide

Questions 1–11 (SG pp. 134–137)

1. Answers will vary depending on class data.

2. Answers will vary. The means from some groups might match. Others should be "close." Students might mention the range of means recorded.

3. *Answers will vary.

4. **A.** Fold the long strip into 5 equal pieces.
   B. Fold the long strip into 3 equal pieces.

5. Add the measurements and divide by the number of people in the group (the number of values).

6. **A.**

   B. *57 cm
   C. *57 cm

7. **A.** *Answers will vary.
   B. *The mean found using the calculator should be close to the mean found using the strips of paper.

8. **A.** Group 3: 57 cm; Group 4: 52 cm
   B. Group 3:

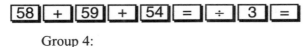

   Group 4:

   C. Group 3: 58 cm; Group 4: 53 cm

9. **A.** 42°

   B. 43°

10. **A.** 2 goals
    B. 2 goals
    C. Yes; Yes

11. **A.** *Answers will vary. median of 13 correct or mean of 15 correct
    B. *

Homework (SG p. 138)

Questions 1–3

1. **A.** 55 inches

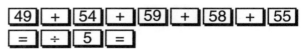

   B. 55 inches
   C. 55 inches
   D. 57 inches
   E. Yes; Yes

2. No; an answer of 12 does not make sense. The four values are 0, 2, 3, and 7. The mean is 3 times. Shannon forgot to divide after adding the four values.

3. **A.** 2 blocks
   B. 3 blocks
   C. Answers will vary. It increases the average. It "pulls up" the average.

Unit Resource Guide

Cookie Factory (URG p. 54)

Questions 1–2

1. **A.** 10 grams
   B. 9.25 grams

*2. **A.** 10 chips
   B. 8 chips
   C. Answers will vary. If the median is used to represent the company's data, then their claim is true. Students may point out that the mean may more accurately represent the data, since the cookies with two chips and five chips will bring this average down.

---

*Answers and/or discussion are included in the Lesson Guide.
**Answers for all the Home Practice in the *Discovery Assignment Book* are at the end of the unit.

K. Drawing Angles (URG p. 14)

Draw an acute angle, a right angle, an obtuse angle, and a 180° angle. Then, switch with a partner and see if he or she can tell which is which.

M. Median (URG p. 15)

Six students grabbed a handful of cubes. They pulled 10, 12, 10, 11, 15, and 14 cubes.

1. What is the median number of cubes in a handful?

2. What is the mean?

O. Bouncing Balls (URG p. 16)

Ming experimented with 3 kinds of balls to find which one bounced the highest. He chose a basketball, a tennis ball, and a kickball. He dropped each ball from 1 meter and measured the bounce height.

1. What is the manipulated variable in Ming's experiment?

2. What is the responding variable?

3. Is the responding variable numerical or categorical?

4. What are the values of the manipulated variable?

5. Name one fixed variable.

Q. Finding Medians (URG p. 17)

In third grade, Luis did an experiment called *Fill 'er Up.* He measured the volume of three different containers.

C Container	V Volume (in cc)			
	Trial 1	Trial 2	Trial 3	Median
Salsa	750 cc	755 cc	760 cc	
Baby Food	98 cc	118 cc	115 cc	
Mayonnaise	1010 cc	1020 cc	1012 cc	

Find the median volume for each container.

DPP Tasks and Challenge are on pages 64–65.
Suggestions for using the DPPs are on pages 64–65.

LESSON GUIDE
Bouncing Ball

Estimated Class Sessions: 4–5

Students use the TIMS Laboratory Method to investigate the relationship between the drop height and bounce height of a tennis ball and a Super ball. Students drop each ball from three different heights and record the bounce height. They take three trials at each drop height and find the average bounce height. They then graph the data and use the graph to make predictions. This lab introduces students to the terms *manipulated variable* and *responding variable.* In this case, the manipulated variable is the drop height. The responding variable is the bounce height.

Key Content

- Measuring length in centimeters.
- Identifying and using variables in an experiment.
- Using patterns in tables and graphs to make predictions and solve problems.
- Collecting, organizing, graphing, and analyzing data.
- Making and interpreting point graphs.
- Drawing best-fit lines.

Key Vocabulary

best-fit line
fixed variable
manipulated variable
responding variable

Curriculum Sequence

Before This Unit

Variables. Students used the TIMS Laboratory Method to investigate the relationship between two numerical variables in Units 1 and 2 in the labs *Arm Span vs. Height* and *Perimeter vs. Length.*

After This Unit

Variables. In this lab students are introduced to the terms manipulated variable and responding variable. Students will identify the manipulated and responding variables in labs they will encounter later in the year (see Units 8, 10, 14, 15, and 16).

Materials List

Print Materials for Students

		Math Facts and Daily Practice and Problems	Lab	Homework	Written Assessment
Student Books	**Student Guide**		*Bouncing Ball* Pages 139–144 and Student Rubric: *Solving* Appendix B and Inside Back Cover (optional) ⊚	*Bouncing Ball* Homework Section Page 145	
	Discovery Assignment Book				Home Practice Part 6 Page 56
Teacher Resources	**Facts Resource Guide** ⊚	DPP Items 5L, 5N & 5P			
	Unit Resource Guide	DPP Items K–R Pages 14–17 ⊚			
	Generic Section ⊚		*Centimeter Graph Paper,* 4 per student and *Three-trial Data Table,* 2 per student		

⊚ *available on Teacher Resource CD*

All Transparency Masters, Blackline Masters, and Assessment Blackline Masters in the Unit Resource Guide are on the Teacher Resource CD.

Supplies for Each Student

ruler

Supplies for Each Student Group

tennis ball (used or new)
Super ball
2 metersticks
masking tape

Materials for the Teacher

Bouncing Ball Data: What's Wrong Here? Transparency Master (Unit Resource Guide) Page 68
TIMS Multidimensional Rubric (Teacher Implementation Guide, Assessment section), optional
Observational Assessment Record (Unit Resource Guide, Pages 7–8 and Teacher Resource CD)

Before the Lab

A drawing of the lab setup is shown in Figure 6. You will need a lab setup for each group of three students. For each group, tape two metersticks to the wall vertically, one on top of the other, with the 100 cm mark at the top of each meterstick. If you cannot find many places on the walls in your classroom to tape two metersticks, tape them to door jambs or on the walls in the hall.

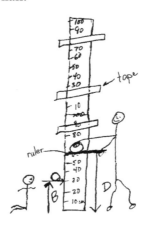

Figure 6: *Lab setup for* Bouncing Ball

It is important that student groups use the same ball to collect the data and check their predictions. Number each ball with a permanent marker so that students can find and use the same ball on succeeding days of the lab.

TIMS Tip

Used tennis balls work as well as or better than new ones. High school or other tennis teams often have a surplus of used tennis balls that work well in this lab. One way to obtain free tennis balls is to ask a coach if he or she is willing to donate them.

Developing the Lab

Part 1. Defining the Variables and Drawing the Picture

To introduce the lab, read the opening vignette on the *Bouncing Ball* Lab Pages in the *Student Guide*. One of the important aspects of this lab is the identification of the **manipulated variable,** the **responding variable,** and the controlled, or **fixed variables.** Use the discussion in the Identifying the Variables section on the *Bouncing Ball* Lab Pages to introduce these terms to your class.

Bouncing Ball

Ana and Tanya wanted to play jacks at lunch time. Tanya brought jacks from home, but forgot the ball. Mrs. Dewey told the girls that they could look for a ball in the closet where the class keeps playground equipment. They found an old tennis ball and a Super ball.

Ana said, "I'll use the Super ball and you can use the tennis ball."

"No, that wouldn't be fair," said Tanya. "The balls won't bounce the same. We have to use the same ball."

"Oh, you're right. Which one should we use?" Ana began to bounce the balls to try them out. "They both bounce pretty well when I drop them from here, but when we play jacks we are sitting down."

Mrs. Dewey said, "You girls better go outside and get your game started or lunch will be over. Experiment with both of the balls before you start to play. You've given me an idea for an experiment we can do in class."

After lunch, Mrs. Dewey asked Tanya and Ana to let her have the tennis ball and the Super ball. She asked the class, "Can you predict how high the tennis ball will bounce if I drop it from 1 meter?"

Students answered:

"One meter."

"Yeah, one meter."

"Half as high. 50 centimeters."

"Higher than a meter."

Student Guide - Page 139

If your students have done experiments in previous grades, as well as the labs in Unit 1 (*Arm Span vs. Height*) and Unit 2 (*Perimeter vs. Length*), they should be familiar with most aspects of the laboratory method. However, the use of the terms manipulated and responding variable will be new to all students.

Use the following discussion prompts to help students identify these variables and understand the steps in the lab. (Figure 6 shows a student drawing of the experimental setup.)

Show the class the lab setup. Ask:

- *If I give you a drop height, do you think you can predict how high the ball will bounce in centimeters?*

As you drop the tennis ball from various heights, ask:

- *Can you predict how high the ball will bounce? Does the ball bounce higher than the drop height? As high as the drop height? Lower than the drop height? Half as high as the drop height?*

- *What would help us make accurate predictions?* (Try out the balls. Test some drops. Measure the bounces. Collect some data. Do an experiment.)

- *In our experiment, we will drop the ball from different heights and then measure the bounce height. What are the two main variables?* (The drop height and the bounce height.)

- *How many drop heights should we try? What should those heights be?* (Depending on the experience of your students, you may or may not want to let them choose the drop heights. To be able to make accurate predictions, students will need to use at least three drop heights that are high enough so that they can accurately measure the bounce height. The heights recommended in the *Student Guide* are 40 cm, 80 cm, and 120 cm. See the Content Note for a discussion about choosing values for the manipulated variable.)

Mrs. Dewey said, "Are you guessing? Or, can you give a reason for your answers? How can we make accurate predictions?"

Jessie said, "We'd have to try it out. We'd have to write down where we want to drop the ball. Then, drop the ball and measure how high it bounces."

Mrs. Dewey said, "Here is the challenge: If I give you a drop height, can you predict the bounce height? Can you make a prediction that is close to the actual bounce height?"

You will use the TIMS Laboratory Method to carry out two experiments: one with a tennis ball and one with a Super ball. Using the results of your experiments, you should be able to accurately predict the bounce height of either ball, if you know the drop height.

Identifying the Variables

One of the first tasks in setting up an experiment is identifying the variables. The two main variables in these two experiments are the drop height (*D*) and the bounce height (*B*).

We have special names for the two main variables in any experiment. The variable with values we know at the beginning of the experiment is called the **manipulated variable.** We can often choose the values of the manipulated variable. The variable with values we learn by doing the experiment is called the **responding variable.**

The values for the manipulated and responding variables change during an experiment. In these experiments, good values for the drop height (*D*) are 40 cm, 80 cm, and 120 cm. Each time you change the drop height, you measure the bounce height (*B*).

140 SG · Grade 4 · Unit 5 · Lesson 4   **Bouncing Ball**

Student Guide - Page 140

Content Note

Choosing Values for the Manipulated Variable. Good choices of values for the manipulated variable allow students to see patterns in the data. Choosing values for the manipulated variable that are multiples of the lowest value allows students to see corresponding patterns in the values of the responding variable. For example, if the drop height doubles, students will be able to see if the bounce height doubles as well. This is clearly shown in the sample data in Figure 8.

Each experiment should tell you how much the bounce height changes when you change the drop height. Usually there are other variables involved in an experiment. Look at the experimental setup. Try bouncing a ball on the floor a few times. What could change the bounce height, besides the drop height? List some.

The variables in your list should remain the same during an experiment, so that the only thing that affects the bounce height is the drop height. These variables are called **fixed variables**. The results of a carefully controlled experiment will help you make accurate predictions.

1. What is the manipulated variable in both the tennis ball experiment and the Super ball experiment?
2. What is the responding variable?
3. What are the fixed variables in each of the experiments?
4. A. Is the bounce height a categorical or numerical variable?
   B. Is the drop height a categorical or numerical variable?
   C. Is the type of ball a categorical or numerical variable?
5. Mrs. Dewey's class dropped the ball three times from each drop height and measured the bounce height each time. Why is it a good idea to do three trials?

Draw a picture of the lab. Show the tools you will use. Be sure to label the two main variables. A student from another class should be able to look at your picture and know what you are going to do during the lab.

Bouncing Ball

SG · Grade 4 · Unit 5 · Lesson 4 **141**

Student Guide - Page 141

Content Note

Manipulated, Responding, and Fixed Variables.

In simple experiments, students look for the relationship between two main variables. We call these two variables the manipulated variable and the responding variable. These variables are also commonly called the independent and dependent variables. After many years of working with students on identification of variables, we have found the terms manipulated and responding to be less confusing than independent and dependent. However, the important idea is for students to understand that as we change the values for the manipulated variable, we look for a corresponding change (a response) in the values of the responding variable.

The idea of controlled, or fixed, variables in an investigation is also very important. In this lab, students change the drop heights and look for corresponding changes in the bounce heights. They try to keep the other variables—type of ball, type of floor, and method of release—constant. If we observe differences in data and only one variable has changed, then we can say with some certainty that the changed variable is probably the cause of the change in the data.

At this point you can incorporate *Questions 1–5* in the *Student Guide* into the class discussion. If students have trouble answering the first three questions, you can rephrase them as suggested below:

- *The two main variables in an experiment are called the manipulated and responding variables. The **manipulated variable** is the variable with values we know at the beginning of the experiment. Which variable, the drop height or the bounce height, is the manipulated variable in this experiment?* (The drop height. *Question 1*)

- *The **responding variable** is the variable with values we learn by doing the experiment. What is the responding variable?* (The bounce height. *Question 2*)

- *What other variables might affect the bounce height besides the drop height? What should stay the same in the experiments so that we know that the change in the bounce height is due to the drop height? What things should stay the same so that the experiments are fair?* (The type of ball will be the same in each experiment. The surface of the floor. The way we drop the ball—dropping it gently, not adding any force. The same ball should be used for each trial. *Question 3*)

Once students can identify the variables and understand the procedure, they are ready to draw a picture. A student's picture is shown in Figure 7. Note that this student clearly identified the manipulated and responding variables and showed the three values for the drop height.

Figure 7: *Student drawing of the experiment*

Part 2. Collecting and Recording the Data

Each student needs two copies of the *Three-trial Data Table*—one for the tennis ball experiment and one for the Super ball experiment. (See Figure 8 for appropriate headings. Students may use the data table provided in the Collect section of the *Bouncing Ball* Lab Pages as a guide for setting up their data tables.)

Three students per group work well in this situation. One student can drop the ball; one can read the bounce height; and one can record the data. Before groups begin collecting data, review the variables that need to be held fixed and model techniques for measuring the bounce height accurately:

• Just release the ball. Do not throw it down.

• Measure the drop height and the bounce height to the bottom of the ball. (See Figure 6.) The student who drops the ball can ensure that the bottom of the ball is at the drop height by placing a ruler at the drop height. The student who is measuring the bounce height needs to kneel down until the ball is at eye level. The student will have to read the meterstick to estimate the bounce height (i.e., the distance from the floor to the bottom of the ball at its highest point). This is tricky and the group should practice a few times before recording the measurements for three trials.

• Carry out three trials for each drop height. That is, for each value of the drop height we drop the ball and measure the bounce height three times. Good experimenters check to be sure they have obtained reasonable values in an experiment by taking more than one measurement. See *Question 5.* In an experiment like this one, the results will rarely be identical, but if they are close we can be reasonably sure that they are correct. Taking several practice bounces before collecting data at each drop height will help students get a feel for the proper range for the data.

• Display and discuss the *Bouncing Ball Data: What's Wrong Here?* Transparency Master. This transparency shows two student data tables that illustrate data collection errors. In the first data table, the group recorded identical values for all three trials for all three drop heights. These results are highly unlikely. Assure students that differences in measurements are expected and encourage them to record their data accurately. The second data table shows realistic data. However, Trial 2 for the 120 cm drop height is not close enough to the measurements in Trials 1 and 3. If this group had taken a few practice bounces before recording their data,

Content Note

What's Close? In an experiment with multiple trials, we expect repeated trials to give measurements that are "close." One difficulty with this idea is that "close" is not a precise mathematical term. The problem of defining "closeness" is dealt with in the section entitled "What's Close?" in the TIMS Tutor: *Estimation, Accuracy, and Error* in the *Teacher Implementation Guide*. In the tutor, we develop the idea of using percentage as a measure of closeness. For example, in Unit 6, an optional lesson introduces 10% as one benchmark for closeness. In other words, we can say that two numbers are close if one differs from the other by less than (approximately) 10%. Since your students are not familiar with using percent, you can let them decide on their own standards or follow a standard you set for closeness. For example, you might specify that the smallest and largest measurements only differ by 10 cm. If measurements fall outside this range, students should take another trial and choose the closest three values for their data. Alternatively, you can use the 10% guideline for closeness. For example, if the bounce heights are around 60 cm, you can specify that the largest and smallest bounce heights (of the three trials) differ from the middle one by less than 6 cm.

Tennis Ball

D Drop Height (in cm)	B Bounce Height (in cm)			
	Trial 1	Trial 2	Trial 3	Average
40	21	20	22	21
80	46	47	43	45
120	61	65	60	62

Super Ball

D Drop Height (in cm)	B Bounce Height (in cm)			
	Trial 1	Trial 2	Trial 3	Average
40	31	32	32	32
80	61	59	61	60
120	93	92	89	91

Figure 8: *Sample data tables for the Tennis Ball and Super Ball experiments*

Work with your group to collect the data for each experiment. You will need two data tables, one for each type of ball.

- Tape two metersticks to the wall. Your teacher will show you how.
- Fill in the values for the drop height before starting. Follow the example.
- For each drop height, do three trials. Find the average bounce height for each trial. Record the average in the data table.

Tennis Ball

D Drop Height (in cm)	B Bounce Height (in cm)			
	Trial 1	Trial 2	Trial 3	Average
40				
80				
120				

Graph

- Make a point graph of your data for each experiment. Use two pieces of graph paper.
- Put the drop height (*D*) on the horizontal axis. Put the bounce height (*B*) on the vertical axis.
- Use the same scales on both graphs. Leave room for extrapolation.
- Remember to title the graphs, label the axes, and include units.
- Plot the average bounce height for each drop height.

142 SG · Grade 4 · Unit 5 · Lesson 4   Bouncing Ball

Student Guide - Page 142

they might have seen that most of their trials resulted in bounce heights between 60 cm and 70 cm, so 85 cm is not reasonable.

- Each group should use the same ball for all trials and predictions. Each ball should be numbered so that groups can find their balls to make predictions or finish taking data on succeeding days of the experiment.

- Each group will find the average of the three trials and record them in the appropriate column in the data table. The mean or the median can be used to find the average. The median is usually easier for the students to find. They can use a calculator to find the mean, but encourage them to give the mean to the nearest whole centimeter. To discuss the use of the mean to average the values from the three trials, use the *Bouncing Ball Data: What's Wrong Here?* Transparency Master again. Ask:

  - *Which average (the median or the mean) is shown in the last column of the second data table?* (The mean because the averages are not the middle values.)

  - *How does the value of 85 cm affect the mean?* (The measurement of 85 cm raises the average, so that it is greater than the other two values.)

  See the TIMS Tutor: *Averages* for more information on means and medians. Sample data tables for both the Tennis Ball and Super Ball experiments are shown in Figure 8. The averages are the means of the three trials for each drop height. To avoid confusion students should indicate on their data tables which average they used.

Part 3. Graphing the Data

Students graph the drop heights and average bounce heights for each type of ball. Students make point graphs for the tennis ball data and Super ball data on separate sheets of graph paper, but they should use the same scale for both graphs so that the graphs can be compared. Students should choose what scale to put on their axes, but remind them that they need to leave room for extrapolation. Scaling by tens on the horizontal axis and by fives on the vertical axis will make accurate predictions possible. Figure 9 shows a sample graph for the tennis ball experiment and Figure 10 shows a sample graph for the Super ball experiment. Note that students should add a point at (0,0) (*Question 6*) and draw a best-fit line on each graph (*Question 7*).

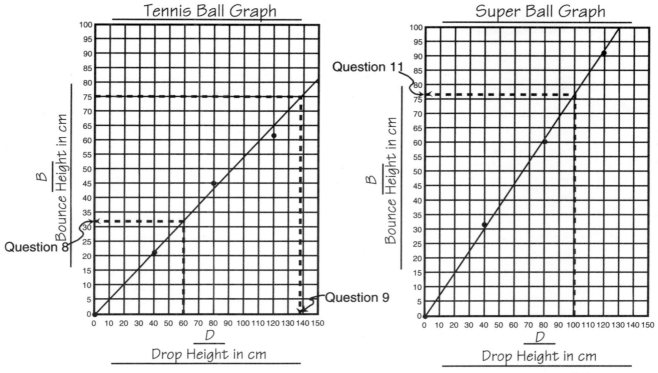

Figure 9: *Sample graph of the tennis ball experiment*

Figure 10: *Sample graph of the Super ball experiment*

Part 4. Exploring the Data

Questions 8–11 ask students to make predictions using their data and then to check the predictions using the same equipment. We recommend that groups make their predictions for all three questions first, then check them all at one time. Before students return to the equipment to check their predictions, ask the class to make a list of all the variables that must be held fixed as they drop the balls and measure the bounce heights. Using the same ball is especially important.

Question 8A asks students to predict the bounce height of their tennis balls if they are dropped from a height of 60 cm. As shown on the sample graph in Figure 9 with dotted lines and arrows, one student predicted that his ball would bounce to a height of 32 cm. This is interpolation since 32 cm lies between the data points on the graph (*Question 8B*). To check the prediction (*Question 8C*), students should drop the same ball from 60 cm and measure the bounce height. *Question 8D* asks if the predicted height is close to the actual bounce height. If, for example, the actual bounce height is 34 cm, the prediction is indeed "close." In this example, predictions from about 31 cm to 37 cm could be considered close to the actual height of 34 cm. See the Content Note in Part 2 for a discussion of "What's Close?"

6. A. If the drop height were 0 cm, what would the bounce height be?
   B. Put this point on your graphs.

7. Describe your graphs. Do the points lie close to a straight line? If so, use a ruler to draw best-fit lines.

8. Suppose you drop your tennis ball from 60 cm.
   A. Use your graph to predict how high it will bounce. D = 60 cm, predicted B = ? Show your work using dotted lines on your graph.
   B. Did you use interpolation or extrapolation to find your answer?
   C. Check your prediction by dropping the tennis ball from 60 cm. What is the actual bounce height? D = 60 cm, actual B = ?
   D. Is your prediction close to the actual bounce height?

9. Suppose you want your tennis ball to bounce 75 cm.
   A. From what height should you drop it? B = 75 cm, predicted D = ?
   B. Did you use interpolation or extrapolation to find your answer?
   C. Check your prediction by dropping the tennis ball from your predicted drop height. What is the actual bounce height?
   D. Was the actual bounce height close to 75 cm?

10. Suppose you drop your tennis ball from 180 cm.
    A. Predict the bounce height. D = 180 cm, predicted B = ?
    B. How did you make your prediction?
    C. Check your prediction by dropping the tennis ball from 180 cm. What is the actual bounce height? D = 180 cm, actual B = ?
    D. Is your prediction close to the actual bounce height?

Bouncing Ball   SG · Grade 4 · Unit 5 · Lesson 4   143

Student Guide - Page 143

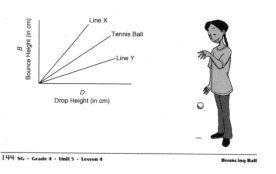
11. Suppose you drop your Super ball from 1 meter.
    A. Use your graph to predict the bounce height. $D = 1$ m, predicted $B = ?$
    B. Did you use interpolation or extrapolation to find your answer?
    C. Check your prediction by dropping the Super ball from 1 m. What is the actual bounce height? $D = 1$ m, actual $B = ?$
    D. Is your prediction close to the actual bounce height?

12. Suppose you want your Super ball to bounce exactly 2 m. From what height should you drop the ball? Explain how you found your answer.

13. Compare the graph for the tennis ball with the graph for the Super ball. How are they alike? How are they different?

14. You find a strange ball on the playground. Because you have been investigating bouncing balls, you drop the ball from a height of 50 cm. It bounces back to a height of 18 cm. Is it more like the tennis ball or the Super ball? How did you find your answer?

15. Maya brings in a ball which is not as lively as a tennis ball. Is the line for Maya's ball Line X or Line Y?

144 SG · Grade 4 · Unit 5 · Lesson 4   Bouncing Ball

Journal Prompt

Did your group work together cooperatively? Describe something someone in your group said that helped your group work together better.

Daily Practice and Problems:
Tasks and Challenge for Lesson 4

L. Task: Area and Perimeter

(URG p. 14)

1. Imagine a rectangle with 7 rows of square-inch tiles. Each row has 7 tiles in it.

   A. What is the area of this rectangle?

   B. What is the perimeter? Make a sketch of this rectangle.

2. Imagine a square with perimeter of 32 inches. What is the area of this square? Make a sketch of this square.

In **Question 9A,** students are asked to predict the drop height of their tennis balls when the bounce height is 75 cm. This is extrapolation (**Question 9B**) since 75 cm is beyond the original data points. The graph in Figure 9 shows the extrapolation process which begins at 75 cm on the vertical axis and ends at 139 cm on the horizontal axis. If a student checked the prediction (**Question 9C**), by dropping the same ball from 139 cm and the ball bounced to 70 cm, the actual bounce height of 70 cm would be considered close to 75 centimeters. Actual bounce heights from 68 cm to 82 cm could be considered close.

Questions 10 and 12 ask students to make predictions about heights which are probably not on the graph. They will have to devise different strategies for solving these problems. The following paragraph is a student response to **Question 12.** Many other strategies are possible. Ask students to share theirs with the class.

> "I knew that if it bounced to 1 meter the drop height would be 130, but I needed 2 meters so I doubled it and I got 260."

Questions 13–15 can be used as part of a final whole-class discussion of the lab. These questions challenge students to think critically about what they have learned. Here is a student's answer for **Question 14:**

> "The tennis ball. I think the tennis ball because on the graph I put my finger on 50 cm at the bottom and I went up and the tennis ball was closer to 18 cm than the super ball."

Suggestions for Teaching the Lesson

Math Facts

DPP Task L provides practice with the math facts for the square numbers by finding areas of squares. Task N provides practice with the square numbers using number sentences with unknowns. Challenge P is a math riddle that uses square numbers.

Homework and Practice

- Assign the Homework section on the *Bouncing Ball* Lab Pages in the *Student Guide.* Note that students will need a piece of *Centimeter Graph Paper* and a ruler to solve the problems.

- Assign the problems *Speeds at the Indianapolis 500* (Lesson 7 in the *Student Guide*) for homework. Students may be interested in looking up recent winning speeds at the Indianapolis 500 in an almanac or on the internet.

- DPP Bit K is a review of acute, obtuse, and right angles. Items M, Q, and R provide practice finding averages. Bit O reviews identification of variables.
- Part 6 of the Home Practice provides more practice on the main ideas of this lesson and can be assigned as homework.

Answers for Part 6 of the Home Practice can be found in the Answer Key at the end of this lesson and at the end of this unit.

Assessment

- Introduce the TIMS Student Rubric: *Solving,* found in Appendix B in the *Student Guide.* This rubric sets goals for good problem-solvers. As students complete **Questions 10** and **12,** use the rubric to help them solve the problem. Refer to this rubric as you comment on their written work. Students will use the *Solving* rubric to guide their work on the assessment problem in Lesson 6 *Professor Peabody Invents a Ball.* The teacher's version of this rubric, the Solving dimension of the *TIMS Multidimensional Rubric,* can be found in the Assessment section in the *Teacher Implementation Guide.*
- Use this lab to assess students' graphing skills. Grade students' graphs based on the following criteria:
  1. Does the graph have a title?
  2. Are the axes scaled correctly and labeled clearly? Labeling should be consistent with the picture and the data table and should include appropriate units of measure.
  3. Are the points plotted correctly?
  4. Did the student correctly draw a best-fit line with a ruler?
  5. Did the student show any interpolation or extrapolation on the graph?
- Use the *Observational Assessment Record* to record students' abilities to fit a best-fit line to a set of data points and measure length in centimeters.
- Place students' work from all or part of this lab in their collection folders. Their work will be used in the *Experiment Review* in Unit 8.
- Use Home Practice Part 6 *Bouncing Balls* as an individual assessment of students' abilities to find medians, identify variables, and graph data.

Answers for Part 6 of the Home Practice can be found in the Answer Key at the end of this lesson and at the end of this unit.

N. Task: Square Numbers (URG p. 15)

Find a number for n that makes each sentence true.

1. $n \times n = 81$ $n =$ ___
2. $n \times n = 36$ $n =$ ___
3. $n \times n = 49$ $n =$ ___
4. $n \times n = 25$ $n =$ ___
5. $n \times n = 9$ $n =$ ___
6. $n \times n = 64$ $n =$ ___
7. $n \times n = 16$ $n =$ ___
8. $n \times n = 1$ $n =$ ___
9. $n \times n = 4$ $n =$ ___

P. Challenge: Another Number Puzzle (URG p. 16)

I am a number between 6 and 150.

I am one more than a square number.

The sum of my digits is a multiple of 5.

I am prime.

What number am I?

Explain your strategy.

R. Task: Finding Means (URG p. 17)

In third grade, Luis did an experiment called *Fill 'er Up.* He measured the volume of three different containers.

C Container	V Volume (in cc)			
	Trial 1	Trial 2	Trial 3	Mean
Salsa	750 cc	755 cc	760 cc	
Baby Food	98 cc	118 cc	115 cc	
Mayonnaise	1010 cc	1020 cc	1012 cc	

Use a calculator to find the mean volume for each container. Give your answer to the nearest cubic centimeter. Look back at your answers. Are they reasonable?

Homework

You will need a piece of *Centimeter Graph Paper* and a ruler to complete this homework.

Here are the results of an experiment using a ball Frank found on the way to school:

1. Make a point graph of this data. Put the drop height (*D*) on the horizontal axis and the bounce height (*B*) on the vertical axis. The scale on the horizontal axis should go to at least 150 cm. The scale on the vertical axis should go to at least 100 cm.

2. A. If the drop height were 0 cm, what would be the bounce height?
   B. Put this point on your graph.

3. Draw a best-fit line.

4. Frank dropped his ball from 150 cm.
   A. Use your graph to predict the bounce height of the ball. Show how you found your answer on your graph. *D* = 150 cm, predicted *B* = ?
   B. Did you use interpolation or extrapolation to find your answer?

5. Frank dropped his ball and it bounced 25 cm.
   A. From what height was it dropped? Show how you found your answer on your graph. *B* = 25 cm, predicted *D* = ?
   B. Did you use interpolation or extrapolation to find your answer?

6. Frank wants his ball to bounce to a height of 100 cm. From what height should he drop the ball? Explain how you found your answer.

Frank's Data

D Drop Height in cm	*B* Bounce Height in cm
30	11
60	18
120	44

Bouncing Ball   SG · Grade 4 · Unit 5 · Lesson 4   145

Suggestions for Teaching the Lesson (*continued*)

Software Connection

Students can use a graphing program such as *Graph Master* to enter the data from the lab and then make a graph. *Graph Master* and other programs will draw a best-fit line. Some programs will plot the points and the students can then draw the best-fit line. If you use *Graph Master,* students first create a scatter plot. The manipulated variable is the independent variable and the responding variable is the dependent variable. Students should use the data table to enter the three drop heights and the three average bounce heights, as well as (0,0).

Student Rubric: Solving

How does this rubric help you?

It helps me plan strategies, find solutions, and check my work when I solve problems.

In My Best Work in Mathematics:

- I read the problem carefully, make a good plan for solving it, and then carry out that plan.
- I use tools like graphs, pictures, tables, or number sentences to help me.
- I use ideas I know from somewhere else to help me solve a problem.
- I keep working on the problem until I find a good solution.
- I look back at my solution to see if my answer makes sense.
- I look back at my work to see what more I can learn from solving the problem.

442 SG · Grade 4 · Appendix B

Name _____ Date _____

Part 6 **Bouncing Balls**

Grace and her lab partner Michael experimented with 3 kinds of balls to find out which one bounced highest. They dropped each type of ball from the same height. Here is their data.

T Type of Ball	*H* Bounce Height (in cm)			
	Trial 1	Trial 2	Trial 3	Median
Basketball	43	41	45	
Kickball	69	65	67	
Tennis Ball	52	51	51	

1. Find the median bounce height for each type of ball. Complete the table with your answers.

2. What is the manipulated variable? Is it a categorical or numerical variable?

3. What is the responding variable? Is it a categorical or numerical variable?

4. Think about these questions before you graph the median bounce height for each type of ball.
   - What variable will you put on the horizontal axis?
   - What variable will you put on the vertical axis?
   - How will you scale and label the axes?
   - What type of graph is appropriate? A point graph or a bar graph?

56   DAB · Grade 4 · Unit 5   USING DATA TO PREDICT

AT A GLANCE

Math Facts and Daily Practice and Problems

DPP items L, N, and P provide practice with math facts for the square numbers. Item K reviews angle measurement. Items M, Q, and R provide practice finding averages. Item O is a review of terminology.

Before the Lab

Number the tennis balls and Super balls. Set up the lab stations.

Part 1. Defining the Variables and Drawing the Picture

1. Discuss *Questions 1–5* on the *Bouncing Ball* Lab Pages in the *Student Guide.*
2. Discuss the **manipulated, responding,** and **fixed variables** in the lab.
3. Model the procedure.
4. Students draw the picture.

Part 2. Collecting and Recording the Data

1. Review the procedures, reminding students of the variables that should remain constant.
2. Discuss the transparency *Bouncing Ball Data: What's Wrong Here?*
3. Decide with the class whether they will use the median or mean to average the data for the three trials.
4. Students collect the data and complete the data tables.

Part 3. Graphing the Data

Students graph the data for each ball on a separate sheet of graph paper.

Part 4. Exploring the Data

1. In *Questions 6–7,* students add a point at (0,0) and draw a best-fit line.
2. In *Questions 8–12,* students make predictions using the data. They check their predictions for *Questions 8–11.*
3. Introduce the Student Rubric: *Solving* to guide students as they answer *Questions 10* and *12.*
4. Discuss the lab in *Questions 13–15.*
5. Place students' work in their collection folders.

Homework

Assign the Homework section in the *Student Guide.*

Assessment

1. Use the TIMS Student Rubric: *Solving* to guide and evaluate student work on *Questions 10* and *12* of the *Student Guide.* Grade students' graphs.
2. Use the *Observational Assessment Record* to note students' abilities to draw and interpret best-fit lines and measure length in centimeters.
3. Use Part 6 of the Home Practice as an assessment.

Notes:

Bouncing Ball Data: What's Wrong Here?

D Drop Height in cm	B Bounce Height in cm			
	Trial 1	Trial 2	Trial 3	Average
40	29	29	29	29
80	50	50	50	50
120	70	70	70	70

D Drop Height in cm	B Bounce Height in cm			
	Trial 1	Trial 2	Trial 3	Average
40	20	22	20	21
80	41	42	38	40
120	61	85	67	71

Student Guide

Questions 1–15 (SG pp. 141–144)

1. *Drop height

2. *Bounce height

3. *Possible answers: the surface of the floor, the ball, the way the ball is dropped.

4. **A.** numerical
   B. numerical
   C. categorical

5. *

6. **A.** 0 cm
   B. Check that students included the point (0, 0) on their graphs.

7. Answers will vary. The points form a line that goes uphill. See Figures 9 and 10 in Lesson Guide 4 for sample student graphs.

Answers to *Questions 8–10* are based on the sample graph in Figure 9 of Lesson Guide 4.

8. **A.** *Answers will vary. About 32 cm.
   B. *interpolation
   C. *Answers will vary.
   D. *Answers will vary. See Content Note, What's Close? in Lesson Guide 4.

9. **A.** *Answers will vary. About 139 cm.
   B. *extrapolation
   C. *Answers will vary.
   D. *Answers will vary. See Content Note, What's Close? in Lesson Guide 4.

10. **A.** Answers will vary. About 96 cm or 98 cm.
    B. Answers will vary. With drop height of 60 cm, ball bounces to about 32 cm. 180 cm is 3 times 60 cm. So the ball would bounce 3 times as high or about 96 cm. With drop height of 90 cm, ball bounces to about 49 cm. 180 cm is twice 90 cm. The ball would bounce twice as high— about 98 cm.
    C. Answers will vary.
    D. Answers will vary. See Content Note, What's Close? in Lesson Guide 4.

Answers to *Questions 11* and *12* are based on the graph in Figure 10 of Lesson Guide 4.

11. **A.** Answers will vary. About 76 cm.
    B. interpolation; 1 meter = 100 cm
    C. Answers will vary.
    D. Answers will vary. See Content Note, What's Close? in Lesson Guide 4.

12. *Answers will vary. About 260 cm.

13. Answers will vary. Both graphs are lines that go uphill. The line for the Super ball is steeper than the line for the tennis ball. For any given drop height, the bounce height is greater for the Super ball than for the tennis ball.

14. *

15. Line Y

Homework

Questions 1–6 (SG p. 145)

1.

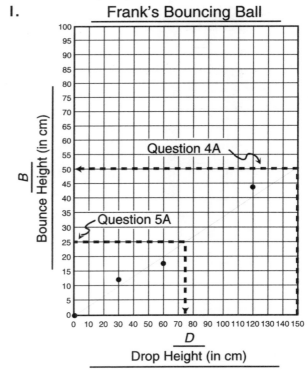

2. **A.** 0 cm
   B. Check that students' graphs include the point (0, 0).

---

*Answers and/or discussion are included in the Lesson Guide.
**Answers for all the Home Practice in the *Discovery Assignment Book* are at the end of the unit.

3. See the graph in *Question 1.*

4. **A.** About 50 cm; See the graph in *Question 1.*
   B. extrapolation

5. **A.** About 75 cm; See the graph in *Question 1.*
   B. interpolation

6. 300 cm; Solution strategies will vary. In *Question 4A* we found that Frank's ball will bounce to about 50 cm when dropped from 150 cm. If we want the bounce height to double from 50 cm to 100 cm, we should double the drop height from 150 cm to 300 cm.

Discovery Assignment Book

**Home Practice (DAB p. 56)

Part 6. Bouncing Balls

Questions 1–4

1. 43 cm, 67 cm, 51 cm

2. Type of Ball, categorical

3. Bounce Height, numerical

4.

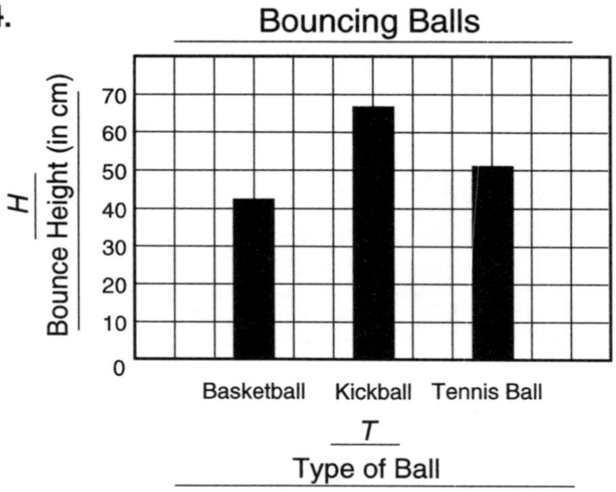

Compare the graphs in Parts 5 and 6 of the Home Practice. When both of the variables to be graphed are numerical as in the 200-meter Backstroke graph in Part 5, a point graph is often the appropriate way to represent the data. Since the values for both of these variables are numbers and since it makes sense to talk about values between the data points, such as 1969, 1970, etc., we can use points and lines. However, in Part 6, it does not make sense to talk about values between the values on the horizontal axis (basketball, kickball, and tennis ball). A bar graph is an appropriate type of graph for representing categorical data. The values (basketball, kickball, and tennis ball) on the graph in Part 6 can also be placed in any order on the graph unlike the numerical values on the horizontal axis in the graph in Part 5. For more information see the TIMS Tutor: *The TIMS Laboratory Method* in the *Teacher Implementation Guide.*

---

*Answers and/or discussion are included in the Lesson Guide.
**Answers for all the Home Practice in the *Discovery Assignment Book* are at the end of the unit.

LESSON GUIDE 5

Two Heads Are Better Than One

Estimated Class Sessions: 1

Two students, Domingo and Sharon, collect data for the *Bouncing Ball* lab. They graph their data and use the graphs to make predictions. When they get two very different answers for one question, they know that one of them has made an error. Together, they review their data and graphs until they are able to find and correct the mistake.

> There are no Daily Practice and Problems items for this lesson.

Key Content

- Working together to solve a problem.
- Looking back to examine the reasonableness of a solution.
- Persisting in the problem-solving process.

Key Vocabulary

best-fit line

Materials List

Print Materials for Students

		Optional Activity	Homework
Student Books	**Adventure Book**	*Two Heads Are Better Than One* Pages 15–28	
	Discovery Assignment Book		Home Practice Part 2 Page 53 (optional)

Adventure Book - Page 16

Adventure Book - Page 17

Below you will find discussion prompts covering many of the ideas in this unit. If you use all the prompts, you may slow the story down so much that the children will not enjoy it. Choose those prompts that best match the needs and interests of your students.

Page 16

* *What experiment are Domingo and Sharon doing?*

The *Bouncing Ball* lab.

* *What is the drop height of the ball?*

80 cm.

Page 17

* *Why does Sharon think it will go to near 60 cm?*

The data table Sharon and Domingo are reviewing shows that for the first two drop heights (40 cm and 80 cm), the ball bounced about half as high (21 cm and 44 cm) as the drop height. Following this pattern, a ball dropped from 120 cm would bounce about 60 cm. Students may have collected similar data in their *Bouncing Ball* labs.

Discussion Prompts

Page 18

- *Does this data table look similar to your data table for the tennis ball experiment? Why or why not?*

- *What patterns do you see in this data table? Did you have similar patterns in your table?*

The bounce height is about half the drop height or the drop height is about twice the bounce height. When the drop height doubled, the bounce height approximately doubled. When the drop height tripled, the bounce height approximately tripled.

- *Did Sharon and Domingo use the median or the mean to average their data?*

They used the median. They chose the middle number for each average.

Adventure Book - Page 18

Page 19

- *Did Sharon and Domingo use interpolation or extrapolation to make their predictions?*

Interpolation.

Adventure Book - Page 19

Adventure Book - Page 22

Adventure Book - Page 23

Discussion Prompts

Pages 22 and 23

- *Look at Sharon and Domingo's lines. Do you think the difference in their predictions could be due to the way they drew their best-fit lines?*

Both lines fit the points reasonably well, so this is probably not the cause of the error.

Discussion Prompts

Page 24

*   *Use the data table on Page 18 to check each data point on the graph. Are they plotted correctly?*

Yes.

*   *Can you find the reason Sharon and Domingo's answers are so far apart?*
*   *Look carefully at the scales on both graphs. Are they correct?*

Adventure Book - Page 24

Page 27

*   *When is it a good idea to work together and when is it better to work alone?*

> **Journal Prompt**
>
> On what kinds of projects or class assignments do you like to work with a partner or a group? When do you like to work alone?

Adventure Book - Page 27

Unit 5: Home Practice

Part 1 Triangle Flash Cards: Square Numbers

Study for the quiz on the multiplication facts for the square numbers. Take home your *Triangle Flash Cards: Square Numbers* and your list of facts you need to study.

Here's how to use the flash cards. Ask a family member to choose one flash card at a time. Your helper should cover the corner containing the highest number. This number will be the answer to a multiplication fact. Multiply the two uncovered numbers.

Your teacher will tell you when the quiz on the square numbers will be.

Part 2 Time and Roman Numerals

A table of Roman numerals is provided in Unit 3 Lesson 2 of your *Student Guide*. You may use it as a reference.

1. Skip count by 3s from 3 to 30 using Roman numerals.

III	VI		XII			XXI			
3	6	9		15					

2. Skip count by 20s from 20 to 200 using Roman numerals.

XX	XL			CXX					
20	40					140			

3. What time does each clock show?

A.   B.   C.

USING DATA TO PREDICT   DAB · Grade 4 · Unit 5   53

Discovery Assignment Book - Page 53

Suggestions for Teaching the Lesson

Homework and Practice

If students completed Unit 3 Lesson 2 *Roman Numerals,* assign Part 2 of the Home Practice.

Answers for Part 2 of the Home Practice can be found in the Answer Key at the end of this lesson and at the end of this unit.

Answer Key • Lesson 5: Two Heads Are Better Than One

Discovery Assignment Book

**Home Practice (DAB p. 53)

Part 2. Time and Roman Numerals

Questions 1–3

1.

III	VI	IX	XII	XV	XVIII	XXI	XXIV	XXVII	XXX
3	6	9	12	15	18	21	24	27	30

2.

XX	XL	LX	LXXX	C	CXX	CXL	CLX	CLXXX	CC
20	40	60	80	100	120	140	160	180	200

3. 3:00, 10:10, 4:40

*Answers and/or discussion are included in the Lesson Guide.
**Answers for all the Home Practice in the *Discovery Assignment Book* are at the end of the unit.

LESSON GUIDE 6

Professor Peabody Invents a Ball

Estimated Class Sessions: 1–2

In this assessment, students use patterns in a data table to make predictions and solve problems. There are many ways for students to answer the questions. The data in the table is similar to the data collected in the lab *Bouncing Ball*. Students use the TIMS Student Rubric: *Solving* as a guide as they devise, carry out, and communicate their problem-solving strategies.

Key Content

- Solving open-ended problems.
- Communicating problem-solving strategies.
- Using patterns in tables and graphs to make predictions.

Daily Practice and Problems: Bit for Lesson 6

S. Paper Towels (URG p. 18)

When Jackie was in the third grade, she did an experiment with paper towels. She dropped water on one sheet of three different brands of paper towels (Ecotowel, Cheap-O, and Handy). She dropped three drops of water on each towel. The water spread out and made a spot. Jackie then measured the area of each spot of water in square centimeters.

1. What is the manipulated variable? What is the responding variable?

2. What are the values of the manipulated variable?

3. Is the manipulated variable numerical or categorical?

4. Name one fixed variable.

DPP Task is on page 86. Suggestions for using the DPPs are on page 86.

Curriculum Sequence

Before This Unit

Using Student Rubrics. Students were introduced to the three student rubrics (*Telling, Solving,* and *Knowing*) in third grade. They used the Student Rubric: *Telling* in Unit 2 of fourth grade.

After This Unit

Using Student Rubrics. Students use the Student Rubric: *Knowing* for the first time in fourth grade in Unit 6. In succeeding units, they continue to use all three student rubrics to guide them as they solve open-response problems.

Materials List

Print Materials for Students

		Math Facts and Daily Practice and Problems	Assessment Activity	Homework	Written Assessment
Student Books	**Student Guide**		Student Rubrics: *Solving* Appendix B and *Telling* Appendix C and Inside Back Cover ◎		
	Discovery Assignment Book			Home Practice Parts 3 & 4 Page 52	
Teacher Resources	**Facts Resource Guide** ◎	DPP Item 5T			
	Unit Resource Guide	DPP Items S–T Page 18 ◎			*Professor Peabody Invents a Ball* Page 88, 1 per student
	Generic Section ◎		*Centimeter Graph Paper,* 1 per student		

◎ *available on Teacher Resource CD*

All Transparency Masters, Blackline Masters, and Assessment Blackline Masters in the Unit Resource Guide are on the Teacher Resource CD.

Supplies for Each Student

ruler
calculator

Materials for the Teacher

TIMS Multidimensional Rubric (Teacher Implementation Guide, Assessment section)
Solving and *Telling* Student Rubric Posters or transparencies of the Student Rubrics: *Solving* and *Telling* (Teacher Implementation Guide, Assessment section)

Developing the Activity

This activity can be used to assess students individually or in groups. To begin, the class reads and discusses the problems on the *Professor Peabody Invents a Ball* Assessment Blackline Master. Students should understand that they are free to devise their own problem-solving strategies and to use any of the tools they normally use in class such as rulers, graph paper, and calculators.

Before students begin working on the problems, review the Student Rubric: *Solving* in Appendix B of the *Student Guide*. You may also review the Student Rubric: *Telling*. Encourage students to write detailed explanations of their problem-solving strategies showing all their steps. To make your expectations clear, inform students that their work will be scored using one or both of the rubrics.

Before assigning scores, give students an opportunity to revise their work based on your comments. For example, if some students use graphs to solve problems, they may need to be reminded to label the axes or to use rulers to draw straight lines. You may need to advise some students to explain how or why they used graphs.

Document the assistance that you give individual students. For example, you might tell students who are having trouble setting up the graph to put the drop height on the horizontal axis and assist them in labeling the axes. However, since they were unable to do this independently, the final score can be lowered.

Students also benefit from a class discussion of exemplary work. While showing a transparency of student work that clearly communicates efficient problem-solving strategies, ask students to critique the work using the student rubrics as guides.

Students should add this assessment to their portfolios and compare their work on *Professor Peabody Invents a Ball* to their work on *A Letter to Myrna* or *Helipads for Antopolis* from Unit 2.

TIMS Tip

Recall that the Student Rubric: *Solving* prepares students for problems which will be scored with the Solving dimension of the *TIMS Multidimensional Rubric*. The Student Rubric: *Telling* prepares students for problems that will be scored with the Telling dimension of the *TIMS Multidimensional Rubric*. These can be found in the Assessment section of the *Teacher Implementation Guide*.

To assist you in scoring your students' work, questions specific to this task are listed below:

Solving

- Did students identify the important elements of the problem? For example, did they know to find the bounce height when given the drop height and find the drop height when given the bounce height?
- Did students organize their work?
- Did students use previously encountered mathematics such as building a table or using a line graph to interpolate and extrapolate?
- Did students persist in the problem-solving process until a solution was reached? Did students look for a second solution strategy to verify the first?
- Did they look back at the problem to check the reasonableness of their results, looking to see if their answers fit the pattern in the original table?

Telling

- Did students clearly describe all their strategies?
- Did they explain why they chose an operation or how their answers fit a pattern in a table or on a graph?
- Did they use appropriate number sentences or other symbolic representations?
- Did they use graphs or data tables to help explain their strategies?
- Did they label their answers with appropriate units (cm) and label their graphs with the appropriate variables?

Samples of student responses to *Questions 1 and 3* are shown below. Four students have been given scores on both the Solving and Telling dimensions of the *TIMS Multidimensional Rubric*. Following the scores for the first two students, you will find examples of the notations teachers made on the *TIMS Multidimensional Rubric* to score the papers. (See Figures 12, 13, 15, and 16.)

Written work from Student A:

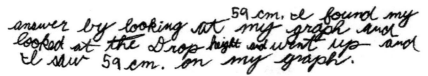

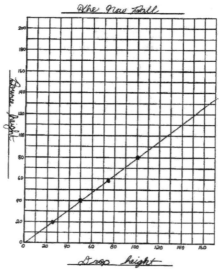

Figure 11: *Sample work for Student A on* ***Question 1***

Solving score: 3

Student A understood the problem in ***Question 1*** and used the graph to predict the bounce height as she did in the experiment *Bouncing Ball*. Her response of 59 cm is a reasonable answer since the error is due to error in drawing the line, not in her method. However, if she had looked back at the table to see if her answer fit the pattern, she might have been able to revise and improve her answer.

Solving	Level 4	Level 3	Level 2	Level 1
Identifies the elements of the problem and their relationships to one another	All major elements identified ✗	Most elements identified	Some, but shows little understanding of relationships	Few or none
Uses problem-solving strategies which are…	Systematic, complete, efficient, and possibly elegant	Systematic and nearly complete, but not efficient ✗	Incomplete or unsystematic	Not evident or inappropriate
Organizes relevant information…	Systematically and efficiently	Systematically, with minor errors ✗	Unsystematically	Not at all
Relates the problem and solution to previously encountered mathematics and makes connections that are…	At length, elegant, and meaningful	Evident ✗	Brief or logically unsound	Not evident
Persists in the problem-solving process…	At length	Until a solution is reached	Briefly ✗	Not at all
Looks back to examine the reasonableness of the solution and draws conclusions that are…	Insightful and comprehensive	Correct	Incorrect or logically unsound ✗	Not present

Figure 12: *Scoring Student A's problem solving on* ***Question 1*** *using the* TIMS Multidimensional Rubric

Telling score: 3

This explanation is reasonably clear. However, if she had been more specific and told us how she knew to read "59 cm" on the vertical axis or indicated this on the graph, we would have a better idea of her method.

Telling	Level 4	Level 3	Level 2	Level 1
Includes response with an explanation and/or description which is…	Complete and clear	Fairly complete and clear	Perhaps ambiguous or unclear	Totally unclear or irrelevant
Presents supporting arguments which are…	Strong and sound	Logically sound, but may contain minor gaps	Incomplete or logically unsound	Not present
Uses pictures, symbols, tables, and graphs which are…	Correct and clearly relevant	Present with minor errors or somewhat irrelevant	Present with errors and/or irrelevant	Not present or completely inappropriate
Uses terminology…	Clearly and precisely	With minor errors	With major errors	Not at all

Figure 13: *Scoring Student A's communication on* **Question 1** *using the* TIMS Multidimensional Rubric

Written work from Student B:

I used my graph and I got 60 cm. even
If I couldn't use a graph I found a way
should go 20,40,60,80,100, and so on.

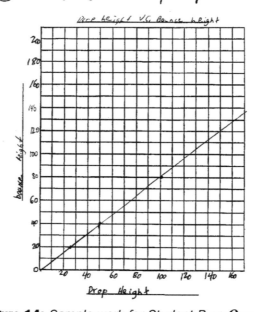

Figure 14: *Sample work for Student B on* **Question 1**

Solving score: 4

Student B used two effective strategies for solving the problem in *Question 1.* He graphed the data and used it to interpolate. Then, he followed the pattern in the data table to find the same answer. Both strategies show that he correctly identified the elements of the problem, finding the bounce height when given the drop height. Using two strategies indicates that he was willing to persist in the problem-solving process and to look back at his first solution to check for the reasonableness of his results by comparing it to the results of the second strategy.

Solving	Level 4	Level 3	Level 2	Level 1
Identifies the elements of the problem and their relationships to one another	All major elements identified	Most elements identified	Some, but shows little understanding of relationships	Few or none
Uses problem-solving strategies which are…	Systematic, complete, efficient, and possibly elegant	Systematic and nearly complete, but not efficient	Incomplete or unsystematic	Not evident or inappropriate
Organizes relevant information…	Systematically and efficiently	Systematically, with minor errors	Unsystematically	Not at all
Relates the problem and solution to previously encountered mathematics and makes connections that are…	At length, elegant, and meaningful	Evident	Brief or logically unsound	Not evident
Persists in the problem-solving process…	At length	Until a solution is reached	Briefly	Not at all
Looks back to examine the reasonableness of the solution and draws conclusions that are…	Insightful and comprehensive	Correct	Incorrect or logically sound	Not present

Figure 15: *Scoring Student B's problem solving on **Question 1** using the* TIMS Multidimensional Rubric

Telling score: 2

Although we have a good idea how Student B solved the problem in **Question 1,** his explanations are not very clear or complete. His graph was correctly labeled and his line was correctly drawn, but he did not show the interpolation on the graph or describe the process. We do not know how he used the graph to come up with an answer of 60 cm. The second part of his explanation indicates that he found a pattern that gave him the correct answer, but he did not tell us how he knew that a 60 cm bounce height corresponded with a 75 cm drop height.

Telling	Level 4	Level 3	Level 2	Level 1
Includes response with an explanation and/or description which is…	Complete and clear	Fairly complete and clear	Perhaps ambiguous or unclear	Totally unclear or irrelevant
Presents supporting arguments which are…	Strong and sound	Logically sound, but may contain minor gaps	Incomplete or logically unsound	Not present
Uses pictures, symbols, tables, and graphs which are…	Correct and clearly relevant	Present with minor errors or somewhat irrelevant	Present with errors and/or irrelevant	Not present or completely inappropriate
Uses terminology…	Clearly and precisely	With minor errors	With major errors	Not at all

Figure 16: *Scoring Student B's communication on **Question 1** using the* TIMS Multidimensional Rubric

Written work from Student C:

250 cm. because I continued the data table on the back of this paper and when the bounce height was 200 cm, it said that the drop height was 250 cm.

Drop hieght	Bounce hieght
125	100
150	120
175	140
200	160
225	180
250	200
275	220
300	240
325	260
350	280
375	300
400	320
425	340
450	360
475	380
500	400

Figure 17: *Sample work for Student C on **Question 3***

Solving score: 3

Student C effectively used table building to help him solve **Question 3.** He knew he had to continue the table to find the drop height when given the bounce height. However, his strategy could have been more efficient since he could have stopped when the bounce height in his table reached 200 cm. We also have no indication that he looked back at his solution to check his results.

Telling score: 4

Student C's explanation and data table are very clear. He explained how the pattern fit in the table and how he used the table to find the drop height given the bounce height.

Written work from Student D:

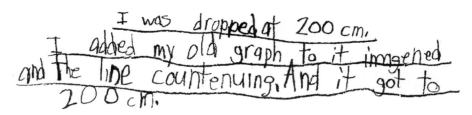

I was dropped at 200 cm. I added my old graph to it imagened and the line countenuing. And it got to 200 cm.

Figure 18: *Sample work for Student D on* ***Question 3***

Solving score: 1

Student D did not identify the important elements of the problem in ***Question 3.*** We are unclear as to whether he was looking for the drop height or the bounce height. His strategy of imagining a line is not effective. Since his result of 200 cm is the same for the value in the question, he did not stop to think about the reasonableness of his results.

Journal Prompt
How can a graph help solve problems?

Telling score: 2

Although Student D's description is unclear as to whether he is looking for a bounce height or drop height and his first sentence is problematic ("I was dropped from 200 cm."), we do have some idea how he attempted to solve the problem. He did attach a graph which could have helped him solve the problem, but he did not use it and his supporting arguments are logically unsound.

Daily Practice and Problems: Task for Lesson 6

T. Task: Missing Factors (URG p. 18) **N**

m and n stand for missing numbers. Find the missing numbers in each of the following.

1. $2 \times m = 4$
2. $m \times 8 = 24$
3. $6 \times m = 36$
4. $10 \times m = 100$
5. $64 \div m = 8$
6. $81 \div 9 = m$
7. $4 \times n = 16$
8. $m \times n = 11$
9. $m^2 = 25$

Suggestions for Teaching the Lesson

Math Facts

DPP Task T provides practice with multiplication and division facts.

Homework and Practice

- DPP Bit S practices identifying variables.
- Assign Parts 3 and 4 of the Home Practice. Part 3 provides practice with prime factors and exponents that can serve as a review of skills that are on the *Midterm Test* in Lesson 8. Part 4 provides practice with addition and subtraction.

Answers for Parts 3 and 4 of the Home Practice can be found in the Answer Key at the end of this lesson and at the end of this unit.

Assessment

Use the *Professor Peabody Invents a Ball* Assessment Blackline Master and the Student Rubrics: *Solving* and *Telling* to assess students' abilities to solve open-response problems and communicate their reasoning.

Name_____ Date _____

Part 3 Factor Trees and Exponents

Write each of the following numbers as a product of prime numbers. If you need more room to show your work, use a separate sheet of paper.

1. 52
2. 85
3. 224

4. Write each of the following using exponents. Then, find each product.
   A. $4 \times 4 \times 2$
   B. $5 \times 2 \times 5$
   C. $2 \times 3 \times 2 \times 2$

Part 4 What's Missing?

The letter n stands for a missing number. What number must n be in each number sentence to make the sentence true?

1. $750 + 150 = n$
2. $839 + 102 = n$
3. $1034 - 40 = n$
4. $2 + n = 100$
5. $16 - n = 8$
6. $n + 21 = 42$
7. $n - 25 = 50$
8. $11 + n = 24$
9. $93 - n = 23$
10. $70 - n = 40$
11. $71 - n = 40$
12. $15 - n = 9$

Discovery Assignment Book - Page 54

AT A GLANCE

Math Facts and Daily Practice and Problems

DPP Bit S reviews identifying variables. Task T provides practice with math facts.

Developing the Activity

1. Students read the problems on the Professor Peabody Invents a Ball Assessment Blackline Master.
2. Advise students that their work will be scored using one or both of the rubrics (Solving and Telling). Review these student rubrics.
3. Students work on the problem individually or in groups and write their explanations.
4. Students revise their work based on your comments.
5. Score the papers using the Solving and Telling dimensions of the TIMS Multidimensional Rubric.
6. Students add their papers to their portfolios.

Homework

Assign Parts 3 and 4 of the Home Practice.

Assessment

Use the Professor Peabody Invents a Ball Assessment Blackline Master to assess problem solving and communication.

Notes:

Name _____   Date _____

Professor Peabody Invents a Ball

Professor Peabody was working for a toy company. His job was to develop a new type of ball. He made a data table of the drop heights and bounce heights he wanted for the new ball.

D Drop Height in cm	B Bounce Height in cm
25	20
50	40
100	80

Solve the following problems. You may use any of the tools that you normally use in class. For example, you may use a ruler, a calculator, or graph paper. Write your answers to the questions on a separate sheet of paper.

1. If the new ball is dropped from a height of 75 cm, how high should it bounce? How did you find your answer?

2. Professor Peabody tested the ball. It worked! When the ball bounced, it followed the pattern in the data table. If the ball bounced to 100 cm, what height was the drop height? Explain how you found your answer.

3. If the ball bounced to 200 cm, what was the drop height? Explain how you found your answer.

Discovery Assignment Book

**Home Practice (DAB p. 54)

Part 3. Factor Trees and Exponents

Questions 1–4

1. $2 \times 2 \times 13 = 52$. Students might draw a factor tree as shown below.

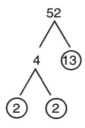

2. $5 \times 17 = 85$. Students might draw a factor tree as shown below.

3. $2 \times 2 \times 2 \times 2 \times 2 \times 7 = 224$. Students might draw a factor tree as shown below.

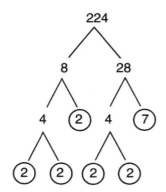

4. **A.** $4^2 \times 2 = 32$
   B. $5^2 \times 2 = 50$
   C. $2^3 \times 3 = 24$

Part 4. What's Missing?

Questions 1–12

1.	900	2.	941
3.	994	4.	98
5.	8	6.	21
7.	75	8.	13
9.	70	10.	30
11.	31	12.	6

Unit Resource Guide

Professor Peabody Invents a Ball (URG p. 88)

Questions 1–3

1. *60 cm. Solution strategies will vary. See samples of student work in the Lesson Guide for possible solutions.

2. 125 cm. Solution strategies will vary. Students might plot a graph for the data and use extrapolation, they might use proportional reasoning, or find patterns in the data table.

3. *250 cm. Solution strategies will vary. See samples of student work in the Lesson Guide for possible solutions.

---

*Answers and/or discussion are included in the Lesson Guide.

**Answers for all the Home Practice in the *Discovery Assignment Book* are at the end of the unit.

OPTIONAL LESSON

There are no Daily Practice and Problems items for this lesson.

LESSON GUIDE 7

Speeds at the Indianapolis 500

Estimated Class Sessions: 1

This lesson is a series of problems concerning the famous annual car race in Indianapolis, Indiana, the Indianapolis 500. Students must solve the problems using skills developed in this unit. They use graphs to make estimates and predictions.

Key Content

- Solving multistep word problems by interpreting and analyzing a set of data.
- Connecting mathematics to real-world situations.
- Communicating solutions verbally and in writing.
- Drawing and interpreting best-fit lines.
- Using patterns in graphs to make predictions.

Materials List

Print Materials for Students

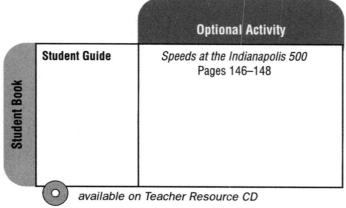

Student Book

Student Guide

Optional Activity

Speeds at the Indianapolis 500
Pages 146–148

⊙ *available on Teacher Resource CD*

All Transparency Masters, Blackline Masters, and Assessment Blackline Masters in the Unit Resource Guide are on the Teacher Resource CD.

Supplies for Each Student

ruler

Developing the Activity

Using Tools. Students may solve the problems in this set using whatever tools work best for them. They will use data in graphs, drawing upon their growing skills interpreting and reading graphs. They may choose to make and use data tables. They may choose calculators, mental math, or paper and pencil for their calculations. A continuing goal is for students to develop a familiarity and comfort level with the tools of mathematics available to them and to develop abilities to use them appropriately and efficiently. For further information, see the TIMS Tutor: *Word Problems* in the *Teacher Implementation Guide.*

Using the Problems. The problems can be used in several ways. Students can work on the problems individually, in pairs, or in groups. One approach is to ask students to work on the problems individually at first and then to come together in pairs or small groups to compare solutions. Then the groups' solutions can be shared with others in a class discussion. The problems can also be assigned for homework. Because this activity does not require much teacher preparation, it is appropriate to leave for a substitute teacher.

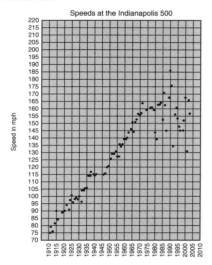

Speeds at the Indianapolis 500

The Indianapolis 500 is a famous car race that takes place every Memorial Day weekend in Indianapolis, Indiana. The cars race around an oval track until they have gone 500 miles. The graph shows the average speed in miles per hour for the winner of each race.

146 SG · Grade 4 · Unit 5 · Lesson 7 — Speeds at the Indianapolis 500

Student Guide - Page 146

The drivers go as fast as possible unless they are given a yellow light. This is a signal that the track is dangerous due to an accident or rain. The cars must slow down and maintain their race position until the track is safe again. When the drivers must drive slower, their average race speeds go down.

1. In 1920 the winner of the race, Gaston Chevrolet, won the race with a winning speed of 89 miles per hour. Fifty years later, Al Unser won with a winning speed of 156 miles per hour. What is the difference in the two speeds?

2. In 1993 the winning speed was 157 miles per hour.
   A. In 1911 the winning speed was 75 miles per hour. About how many times faster did the winner drive in 1993 than in 1911?
   B. The speed limit on freeways in cities is usually 55 miles per hour. About how many times faster did the winning 1993 car travel during the race than a car travels on a freeway?

3. When Jessie's family went on a trip in their car, they drove about 50 miles each hour. How long did it take Jessie's family to drive 500 miles?

4. There were no races in 1917 or 1918 during World War I.
   A. Can you use the graph to estimate the winning speed if there had been a race in 1917? If so, what is your estimate?
   B. Did you use interpolation or extrapolation to make your estimate?

5. There were no races from 1942–1945 during World War II.
   A. Can you use the graph to estimate the winning speed if there had been a race in 1943? If so, what is your estimate?
   B. Did you use interpolation or extrapolation to make your estimate?

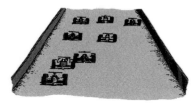

Speeds at the Indianapolis 500 — SG · Grade 4 · Unit 5 · Lesson 7 147

Student Guide - Page 147

---

6. Can you use the graph to make an accurate prediction about the winning speed in 2010? Why or why not?
   A. If so, what is your prediction?
   B. Did you use interpolation or extrapolation?

7. Write a short paragraph that tells the story of the graph. In your paragraph, describe the graph. What does the graph tell you about the speeds of the winning cars over the years?

8. Here is part of the graph. This part shows the winning speeds from 1980 to 2003.

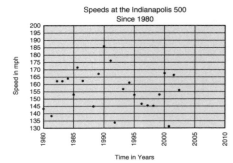

Speeds at the Indianapolis 500 Since 1980

A. Describe this part of the graph.
B. Can you make predictions about the speed of the winner using only this data? Why or why not?

148 SG · Grade 4 · Unit 5 · Lesson 7 — Speeds at the Indianapolis 500

Student Guide - Page 148

This set of word problems utilizes skills students have developed in this unit. Students are given a graph that shows the years and winning times of the Indianapolis 500. They then must interpret the graph to answer questions. They use estimation and computation skills in *Questions 1–2.* They use the data to make predictions for future races and estimates of likely winning times of years in which the race was not held (*Questions 4–6*). They analyze and describe general trends that are apparent in the data (*Question 7*). They analyze portions of the data to determine when it is possible to make predictions and when it is not (*Question 8*).

Suggestions for Teaching the Lesson

Homework and Practice

Assign some or all of the problems on the *Speeds at the Indianapolis 500* Activity Pages for homework.

AT A GLANCE

Developing the Activity

1. Students solve problems on the *Speeds at the Indianapolis 500* Activity Pages in the *Student Guide*.

2. Students discuss solutions and solution paths.

Homework

Assign some or all of the problems for homework.

Notes:

Student Guide

Questions 1–8 (SG pp. 147–148)

1. $156 - 89 = 67$ miles per hour

2. **A.** About 2 times faster.

    B. About 3 times faster.

3. About 10 hours.

4. **A.** Estimates will vary. About 87 miles per hour. Accept estimates between 85 and 90 miles per hour.

    B. Interpolation

5. **A.** Estimates will vary. About 117 miles per hour. Accept estimates between 115 and 120 miles per hour.

    B. Interpolation

6. Answers and explanations will vary. Students should see that the pattern doesn't hold true after about 1980. They may make a prediction using a range. They can predict that the speed will be between 130 and 180 mph.

    A. A possible prediction is about 190 miles per hour.

    B. Extrapolation

7. Answers will vary. Students might say that the graph tends to go uphill at a steady rate until about 1980 when the data becomes rather scattered. Until 1980 the winning speeds increased over the years, with the exception of the war years. After 1980 the winning speeds varied widely.

8. **A.** Answers will vary. Students may say that the points are scattered with no visible pattern.

    B. No, the points do not suggest a line or other pattern with which to make a prediction.

*Answers and/or discussion are included in the Lesson Guide.
**Answers for all the Home Practice in the *Discovery Assignment Book* are at the end of the unit.

Daily Practice and Problems:
Bit for Lesson 8

U. Quiz on the Square Numbers

(URG p. 19)

A. $4 \times 4 =$

B. $7 \times 7 =$

C. $2 \times 2 =$

D. $10 \times 10 =$

E. $3 \times 3 =$

F. $5 \times 5 =$

G. $6 \times 6 =$

H. $8 \times 8 =$

I. $9 \times 9 =$

J. $1 \times 1 =$

DPP Challenge is on page 95. Suggestions for using the DPPs are on page 95.

LESSON GUIDE 8

Midterm Test

Estimated Class Sessions: 1

Students take a paper-and-pencil test consisting of 12 items. These items test skills and concepts studied in the first five units.

Key Content

- Assessing concepts and skills developed since the beginning of the year.

Materials List

Print Materials for Students

		Math Facts and Daily Practice and Problems	Written Assessment
Teacher Resources	**Facts Resource Guide**	DPP Item 5U	DPP Item 5U *Quiz on the Square Numbers*
	Unit Resource Guide	DPP Items U–V Page 19	*Midterm Test* Pages 97–101, 1 per student and DPP Item U *Quiz on the Square Numbers* Page 19

⊙ *available on Teacher Resource CD*

All Transparency Masters, Blackline Masters, and Assessment Blackline Masters in the Unit Resource Guide are on the Teacher Resource CD.

Supplies for Each Student

ruler
calculator
square-inch tiles

Materials for the Teacher

Observational Assessment Record (Unit Resource Guide, Pages 7–8 and Teacher Resource CD)
Individual Assessment Record Sheet (Teacher Implementation Guide, Assessment section and Teacher Resource CD)

Before the Activity

Look over the problems on the test before administering it. If you chose not to complete some of the activities in Units 1–5, omit items from the test that use content from those activities.

Developing the Activity

Students take the test individually. Although the test was designed to take one class session for students to complete, you may wish to give them more time. Part 1 of the test should be completed without any manipulatives or calculators. Collect Part 1 of the test before students begin Part 2. Students will need a ruler and a calculator to complete Part 2 of the test. Square-inch tiles should also be available for students to use, since several of the items ask questions involving the tiles.

Some of the items ask the student to tell how he or she solved the problem. Remind students to give full explanations for their problem-solving strategies.

Suggestions for Teaching the Lesson

Homework and Practice

DPP Challenge V is a variation of the digits game in which students use a given set of digits to make the largest possible sum or the smallest possible sum.

Assessment

- Use the *Midterm Test* to assess students' understanding of the material covered in Units 1 through 5. Include students' tests in their portfolios so that you can compare their work on this test to their work on similar tests in Units 8, 12, and 16.

- DPP Bit U is a short quiz on the math facts for the square numbers.

- Transfer appropriate documentation from the Unit 5 *Observational Assessment Record* to the students' *Individual Assessment Record Sheets*.

Social Studies Connection

The data represented in the graph in *Question 12* is interesting historically. Women first ran in the 800-meter event in the 1928 Olympics. Since some of the women collapsed from exhaustion after the race, Olympic officials decided women should not compete in events longer than 200 meters. The 800-meter women's event was not included in the games again until 1960.

Daily Practice and Problems: Challenge for Lesson 8

V. Challenge: Biggest and Smallest Sums (URG p. 19) **N** **✖**

Put a digit (1, 2, 3, 4, 5, 6, 7, 8, 9, or 0) in each box. Use each digit once or not at all.

☐ ☐ ☐ ☐ + ☐ ☐ ☐ ☐

What is the biggest sum you can make?

What is the smallest?

What if a digit can be used more than once?

Explain your strategies.

Math Facts and Daily Practice and Problems

DPP Bit U is a short quiz on the math facts for the square numbers. Challenge V is an activity that develops number sense and practices multidigit addition.

Developing the Activity

1. Students take Part 1 of the *Midterm Test* using paper and pencil only.
2. Collect Part 1.
3. Students take Part 2 of the *Midterm Test* using calculators, rulers, and square-inch tiles.

Assessment

1. Use the *Midterm Test* to assess students' understanding of concepts in Units 1 through 5. Place students' tests in their portfolios.
2. Use DPP Bit U to assess students' fluency with the multiplication facts for the square numbers.
3. Transfer appropriate documentation from the Unit 5 *Observational Assessment Record* to the students' *Individual Assessment Record Sheets.*

Notes:

Name _____   Date _____

Midterm Test

Part 1

Use paper and pencil to complete the following questions. Estimate to be sure your answer is reasonable.

1. **A.**   326
         + 177

   B.   1583
          + 219

2. **A.**   2107
         − 239

   B.   6490
          − 1627

3. Explain your estimation strategy for Question 2A.

4. **A.** Write 2346 using base-ten shorthand.

   B. What is the value of the 3 in 2346? Tell how you know.

Part 2

As you answer the following questions, you may use any of the tools you have used in class. For example, you may wish to use a ruler, a calculator, or square-inch tiles.

5. This is one square inch.

A. What is the area of the figure below?

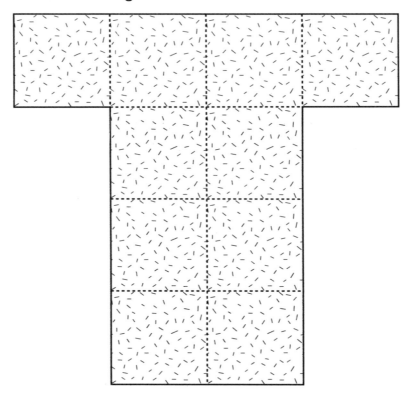

B. What is the perimeter?

6. Grace used square-inch tiles to make a rectangle. Grace's rectangle was 5 inches wide and 12 inches long.

   A. How many square-inch tiles did Grace use to make her rectangle?

   B. What is the perimeter of Grace's rectangle?

7. Tom made a rectangle with 36 tiles. If there are 4 rows, how many tiles are in each row? Show how you found your answer.

8. **A.** Is 4 a factor of 24? Tell how you know.

   B. Is 4 a factor of 27? Tell how you know.

9. Use a factor tree to factor 72 into primes. Write a number sentence to show your answer.

10. Tell whether each of these angles is acute, right, or obtuse:

A.

B.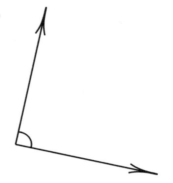

C.

D.

11. The students in Mrs. Dewey's class keep a weekly record of the books they read. Here is Lee Yah's record for the first five weeks:

Lee Yah's Data

Week	Number of Books
1	2
2	5
3	1
4	5
5	2

A. Find the median number of books she read during the 5 weeks.

B. Find the mean.

12. The graph below shows the winning times in the women's 800-meter run in the summer Olympics. The times are given in minutes and seconds. For example, 1:40 means 1 minute and 40 seconds. (800 meters is about one-half mile.)

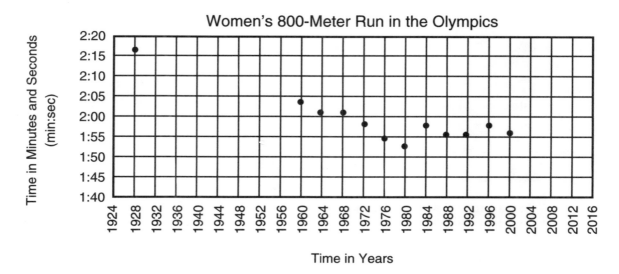

Women's 800-Meter Run in the Olympics

A. Draw a best-fit line for these data points.

B. The first 800-meter women's race was held in the 1928 Olympic Games. The next race was not held until 1960. Estimate the time of the winner if the race had been held in 1952.

C. Did you use interpolation or extrapolation to make your prediction about the race in the year 1952?

Unit Resource Guide

Midterm Test (URG pp. 97–101)

Questions 1–12

1. **A.** 503
   B. 1802

2. **A.** 1868
   B. 4863

3. Answers will vary.
   Possible strategy: $2100 - 200 = 1900$.

4. **A.**

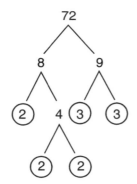

   B. 300. Explanations will vary. The three is for 3 flats each of which has a value of 100.

5. **A.** 10 square inches
   B. 16 inches

6. **A.** $5 \times 12 = 60$ square-inch tiles
   B. $5 + 5 + 12 + 12 = 34$ inches

7. 9 tiles in each row. Solution strategies will vary. $36 \div 4 = 9$.

8. **A.** Yes. 4 divides into 24 evenly, $24 \div 4 = 6$.
   B. No. 4 does not divide into 27 evenly. It has a remainder. $27 \div 4 = 6$ R3.

9. One possible factor tree is shown here. Others are possible. $2 \times 2 \times 2 \times 3 \times 3$ or $2^3 \times 3^2$

10. **A.** Right
    B. Obtuse
    C. Acute
    D. Right

11. **A.** 2 books
    B. 3 books

12. **A.**

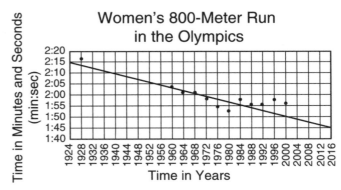

Women's 800-Meter Run in the Olympics

   B. Predictions will vary depending on how the best-fit line is drawn. About 2 minutes and 6 seconds. Accept predictions between 2:00 and 2:10.

   C. Interpolation

---

*Answers and/or discussion are included in the Lesson Guide.

**Answers for all the Home Practice in the *Discovery Assignment Book* are at the end of the unit.

Discovery Assignment Book

Part 2. Time and Roman Numerals

Questions 1–3 (DAB p. 53)

1.

III	VI	IX	XII	XV	XVIII	XXI	XXIV	XXVII	XXX
3	6	9	12	15	18	21	24	27	30

2.

XX	XL	LX	LXXX	C	CXX	CXL	CLX	CLXXX	CC
20	40	60	80	100	120	140	160	180	200

3. 3:00, 10:10, 4:40

Part 3. Factor Trees and Exponents

Questions 1–4 (DAB p. 54)

1. $2 \times 2 \times 13 = 52$. Students might draw a factor tree as shown below.

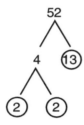

2. $5 \times 17 = 85$. Students might draw a factor tree as shown below.

3. $2 \times 2 \times 2 \times 2 \times 2 \times 7 = 224$. Students might draw a factor tree as shown below.

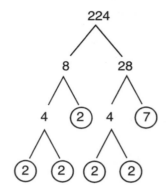

4. **A.** $4^2 \times 2 = 32$
B. $5^2 \times 2 = 50$
C. $2^3 \times 3 = 24$

Part 4. What's Missing?

Questions 1–12 (DAB p. 54)

1.	900	**2.**	941
3.	994	**4.**	98
5.	8	**6.**	21
7.	75	**8.**	13
9.	70	**10.**	30
11.	31	**12.**	6

*Answers and/or discussion are included in the Lesson Guide.

Part 5. Making Predictions from a Graph

Questions 1–7 (DAB p. 55)

1.

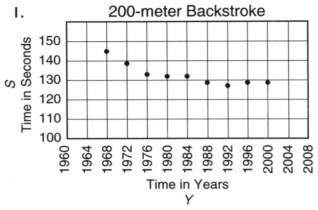

200-meter Backstroke

2. **A.** Time in Years
   B. Numerical
3. Time in Seconds
4. about 2 minutes
5. Yes.

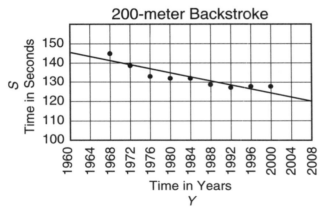

200-meter Backstroke

6. Answers will vary. Students might say that the times are decreasing, the graph is going downhill, or that women are getting to be faster swimmers.

7. *Predictions will vary. About 121 seconds. Accept predictions between 115 and 125 seconds. Discuss that predictions beyond the data are not always reliable.

Part 6. Bouncing Balls

Questions 1–4 (DAB p. 56)

1. 43, 67, 51
2. Type of Ball, categorical
3. Bounce Height, numerical
4.

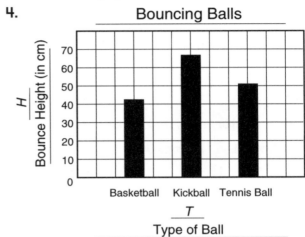

Bouncing Balls

Compare the graphs in Parts 5 and 6 of the Home Practice. When both of the variables to be graphed are numerical as in the 200-meter Backstroke graph in Part 5, a point graph is often the appropriate way to represent the data. Since the values for both of these variables are numbers and since it makes sense to talk about values between the data points, such as 1969, 1970, etc., we can use points and lines. However, in Part 6, it does not make sense to talk about values between the values on the horizontal axis (basketball, kickball, and tennis ball). A bar graph is an appropriate type of graph for representing categorical data. The values (basketball, kickball, and tennis ball) on the graph in Part 6 can also be placed in any order on the graph unlike the numerical values on the horizontal axis in the graph in Part 5. For more information see the TIMS Tutor: *The TIMS Laboratory Method* in the *Teacher Implementation Guide.*

*Answers and/or discussion are included in the Lesson Guide.